A WOMAN'S PLACE IS IN SALES

How to be a Diamond in Party plan sales

By Debbie Bush

A Woman's Place is in Sales
Copyright © 2020 Deborah Bush

ISBN: 9781796240825

Publisher
10-10-10 Publishing
Markham, ON
Canada
Printed in Canada and the United States of America

Table of Contents

DEDICATION

TO TERRY:

    For over 40 years of love, support & understanding

TO ANGELA, TONY, & JANINE

    You are the reason I started a career in party plan, to stay home with you and enjoy your younger years.

TO MOM & DAD

    Thanks for giving me the work ethic that enabled me to be such a success in a business with no boss telling me what to do and when to do it.

FORWARD

Debbie's sales career spans over 25 years. She started selling Tupperware in her 20's to support her family of five while her husband went to college. She found she liked the flexibility of staying with her children during the daytime and doing parties for her income in the evening. Her passion immediately surfaced—working with people. She excelled in customer service, dating parties and bringing new consultants into the company.

Like all salespeople, Debbie had her share of disappointments and dismal sales but her positive attitude carried her through the tough times. She changed companies due to her husband's job relocations; weathered companies going out of business and rebuilt her team several times. She understands the challenges of team management, economy downturns, and company disappointments. But she also knows the benefits of party plan sales far outweigh the negatives.

She managed a sales team of 30 people that consistently ranked in the top 5% in the region and top 10% in the nation. Her monthly sales level awarded her a company car to drive. She recruited and trained a minimum of 4 sales personnel per month and maintained the top recruiter of the region for 18 months. She earned sales award trips to destinations such as Thailand, Italy, Hawaii, & England. In 2003 she earned Top Individual Salesperson in the nation.

In addition to Debbie's sales and recruiting skills, she is an excellent teacher. In two of the party plan companies, she trained consultants as well as managers in sales & recruiting, leadership skills, personal development and time management. She always is ready to help a new consultant who needs help in her new endeavor. Many times Debbie used her travel time to a party, meeting or national convention to explain her methods to another consultant or new manager.

Her chapters are easy to read and the instructions are arranged in step by step order. There are many ideas for new as well as experienced consultants and managers. Everyone who has an interest in party plan sales can gain some knowledge and insight from Debbie's experiences.

Raymond Aaron
New York Times Best Selling Author

ACKNOWLEDGEMENTS

I would like to acknowledge the unwavering support and belief in me that my husband possesses. For all the nights he watched the kids so I could go out to "party". His constant support and prodding for me to finish this book kept me focused on finishing it. Without his confidence and assistance, my achievements would have been significantly lower.

I would like to acknowledge my distributors Frank and Edie Zdep who believed in my sales ability even when I did not. Edie refused to let me give my car back when I wanted to quit. I also want to thank all of my fellow managers, consultants, and distributors in E-Z Distributors. All of you contributed to my success there as well as the sales organizations that followed.

I also want to thank my family for their support in my sales career. Also for editing and reading this book even though it probably was not very interesting to them. It has been a long road to finish this book and I am thankful for anyone who helped me along the way.

Chapter 1
A New Revolution--Party Plan

America's economic foundation is forever intertwined with the entrepreneurial salesman. Door to door salesmen traveled the countryside selling their wares for centuries. In the early 20th century a new method of direct selling made its entry into the direct marketing scene – home parties. Women embraced this new avenue of selling and found they could sell product to earn a little extra money for the family without having to hold a full-time job or be a door to door salesperson. Party plan offered flexibility to control their hours and the amount they wanted to earn. They could be home for the children and still earn money for the budget. The efforts of these early pioneers dramatically influenced the home party sales market that exists today.

Before the existence of party plan, direct sales were predominantly the door-to-door salesman. Somewhere around 90,000 salesmen were selling their wares to homes across America by the beginning of the 20th century. This salesman peddled items such as cure-all potions, bibles, encyclopedias, vacuum cleaners, and cleaning products. Selling door-to-door was an effective way for companies to market their products while minimizing their overhead costs.

The door to door salesman and his customers developed a unique personal relationship. Generally, women stayed at home and bought from his selection of goods. A visit from a salesman was usually a welcome break from the housework and kids. A good salesman cultivated a need or desire for one or more of his products. Many products were consumable such as cleaning products and food. Repeat business was the lifeblood for these salesmen. The salesman sold himself first; the product, second. It did not mean the product could be inferior but as long he offered a good value, the salesman's charisma and customer service helped sell products.

The post war economy boomed. Home sales and consumer spending rose. People moved to the suburbs where there was a sense of community. City life did not promote neighborly BBQs and get-togethers; suburban living did. This shift fueled the new party plan format.

Working class people wanted luxuries such as television sets, washing machines, and vacuum cleaners but their income remained unchanged. Party Plan helped women earn money to buy household appliances and items not possible with current income levels. Although many husbands did not want their wives to work, party plan did not seem like a real job to the men. Ironically, a consultant in party plan could work a few evenings a week and often make almost as much as someone who worked all day. In addition, party plan offered reward programs where consultants brought home additional household items and felt great contributing those luxuries to the household.

Initially, party plan was a business where women could go out a couple of evenings and earn some extra money for the family. However, the more evenings she went out selling product, the more money entered the monthly budget. Once consistent money began to flow into the budget, husbands saw the financial impact those few evenings' work made. It was not a real job but it certainly was bringing in real money. She still did the housework and took care of the kids but at night, she was building her own career. Her confidence grew. She knew her product and earned a good paycheck!

The heyday for party plan sales began in the 1950's and continued throughout the 1970's. In the 70's, the women's rights movement put a huge damper on people hosting parties. A distinct line evolved between the career women and the stay at home mom. The career women felt they escaped the housewife status and the stay at home moms felt they chose their path for the good of the children. Parties continued but attendance and excitement faltered.

The 80's and early 90's saw a transition into an era of technology and fast-paced lifestyle. No one seemed to have time to attend parties. The internet introduced a new marketing venue that required little effort and minimal time. Women could get online at work, order almost anything they needed, and have it delivered directly to their home or workplace. Why should they go to a home party and waste two hours of their evening? Many people dismissed party plan and considered it a dinosaur in the sales world. But they did not consider human connection. Yes, easier and faster ways to buy product now existed but humans crave other human interaction. Re-enter party plan!

In 1991, home party sales began to rise again and continued to rise for the next 18 years. Incredibly, sales doubled from 1995 to 2006. Nothing can compete with the social interaction and community camaraderie that home parties provide. Women needed the connection with their friends and family. Attending a home party filled the social need.

Starting in the 21st century, more and more companies decided to get in on the action of party plan sales. Companies that never marketed in the party plan arena are starting to emulate the party plan ideology. New, successful party plans are forming continually. No matter what the economy, people are always looking for ways to make extra income. Corporations are beginning to see the value of direct selling. It is estimated that 60-80% of a company's yearly budget is spent on advertising and distribution. Party plan reduces the cost of operation while creating direct interaction with the customers. In other words, it increases profitability while also improving customer satisfaction.

If there was ever a perfect career for a woman, it is party plan sales. Why are women so perfect in party plan? From the beginning, home parties immediately appealed to the women for its flexibility and camaraderie. Even today, it continues to be comprised of mainly women. While men are not excluded from party plan, very few have any desire to enter this marketing venue. Party plan embraces the personality traits most women possess. Regardless of gender, it is great career for anyone who believes in team success and the acknowledgement of accomplishments. .

Today, party plan is a place where women can not only find a satisfying job, they can excel. Party plan is definitely a "Great Girls' Club." Women are not held back from management. In fact, they ARE management. Every person in party plan is encouraged to rise to the next level. In party plan, men are the minority and women, the majority.

Chapter 2
Party Plan--A Dream Job?

For many new consultants, finding a career in party plan is an unexpected discovery. It is a unique lifestyle and career choice that many people enjoy and learn to love. Not everyone is compatible with the sales atmosphere. It is a roller coaster ride of overwhelming successes and depressing failures. Those who do find a home with their chosen party plan company would not readily desert it. A sales consultant is an entrepreneur at heart who resists the 9-5 regimen and the boss' watchful eye.

A sales job is often seen as an easy career choice: one that does not require formal education and little or no experience. Few colleges offer a dedicated curriculum to sales and marketing of party plan/direct marketing. Most consultants are women for the simple reason that they constitute the majority of stay at home parents. This kind of job enables them to be home when the kids are and not have to ask the boss for days off when the kids are sick or have activities. If Dad is home in the evening when most parties are held, there is no need for a portion of the paycheck to go to a babysitter.

Consultants begin their career in party plan for many different reasons. They are usually pleasantly surprised that they are able to make good money. While the paycheck satisfies the budget, most consultants do not stay in party plan primarily for the money, they stay for the "extras." These include gifts, bonuses, friendly competition, and pride in accomplishments. Party Plan fulfills dreams. Many achieve a level of success and respect they never believed possible. Some become leaders and people builders, recruiting, managing, training, and motivating new sales people while continuing to sell product themselves.

I held a party to help my aunt who was a manager in a well-known party plan company. I warned my aunt that she was probably wasting her time. My past experience with in home parties consisted of low attendance and sales. Not much reward for either person. To my surprise the party was a success. There were 10 people at the party. We had a lot of fun and the sales were equally as good.

As we were wrapping up the party she proceeded to explain the benefits of becoming a consultant. She used phrases like, "You can work whenever you want; not when the boss tells you to", and "How would you like to make between $20 and $25 per hour?" It sounded great but I had always been a person who became ill at the thought of having to stand up in front of anyone–especially my peers– and talk. I took a failing grade in school to avoid speaking in front of my class.

A better than average party, excitement over the extra free merchandise I had earned, and a large need for money began to melt my resolve. My husband was in school and we had 3 small children so the thought of some free merchandise and added income was very enticing. My fear of speaking in front of people still remained but the potential rewards combined with the safety net of being able to quit after a few parties if I didn't like it started to outweigh my fears. The little voice that kept saying, "There is NO WAY you can do this!!" weakened. All I had to do was 6 parties and I could walk away with the merchandise in the kit and a little extra money. Hmmm.... Even I could do that! My aunt had approached me at the perfect point of financial desperation in my life. A different moment in time and I might have turned her down flat.

My aunt knew I worked as a waitress at night so I could stay home with my kids during the day. My paycheck was not a problem, my hours were. I sometimes worked until 3 am. "Try it for 6 parties. If you don't like it, you can leave." I quieted the negative voice by promising myself to do 6 parties and then leave and continue my current job but that isn't **exactly** how it went.

My first party was with my mom. Thank goodness for mothers. It had to be the worst demonstration any of them had ever witnessed. I use the word demonstration lightly in this case. A five minute talk and in so many words, "Here it is. If you want it, buy it." Amazingly, the people purchased product and even booked parties. Chances are they felt sorry for me. Whatever the reason, they got me started.

At each of my 5 starter parties, at least 2 more parties materialized. My friends and family continued to endure the demonstrations. Slowly, I began to relax and enjoy myself. I couldn't walk away from the new parties I dated at each party. The money started to roll in, then the free gifts based on the sales. One day I realized I liked it! I made the decision to quit my waitress job and devote my time to my new venture.

All my relatives and friends thought I had lost my mind to leave my good paying job for a commission based one. I liked the freedom of being my own boss and I my hourly wage in party plan far surpassed what I currently earned as a waitress.

There were times I almost gave up selling party plan but I kept going. Some paychecks were very lean in the beginning. We ate a lot of spaghetti and peanut butter and jelly. For me it was well worth the sacrifice. I do not encourage anyone to quit their jobs and jump into party plan. Each person must weigh the pros and cons before making such a drastic move.

I made this the first of many successful party plan careers. I put my husband through school with the money I earned and my home was filled with many contest winnings–curio cabinet, clothes dryer, TV, to name a few. I began making terrific money, lots of camaraderie, AND, I could stay home with my children. Does it get any better than that?

To those of you considering joining a party plan, my advice to you is that you have nothing to lose and everything to gain. What is the worst thing that can happen? You do a few parties and end up with free merchandise and money and walk away. The best thing that can happen is that you find a new career that most people have no idea exists. The majority of the population has the attitude that you can't make any money in party plan. I am here to show you how it is possible and how I did.

The most important step when deciding to sell party plan is evaluating the company. Party plan is a unique and different sales technique. Newly established party plans need to be researched thoroughly. Not every new party plan is successful. You do not want to invest time, money and energy in a business that folds in a year or two. While no company comes with a guarantee, there are some qualities to look for and warning signs to watch out for.

There is no guarantee of success with any job, sales or otherwise, but making an informed decision helps. If this is your first time in party plan sales, make sure you do your homework and consider worst case scenarios before committing yourself. Take time to examine the party plan you would like to join.

When evaluating a company, keep 4P's in mind---Product, Program, Positive Energy and People. The absence of any one of these could cause a company to either fail or seriously flounder. Sometimes a company lacks one of these requirements and eventually rectifies the situation. Your time is valuable so make sure to find the best fit for your particular needs and circumstances.

Here are the 4 P's of Party Plan:

Product:
Without a quality product, a party plan cannot survive. The reliability of a product is the foundation on which a company rests. If the product falls apart, is of inferior quality, or is inconsistent, customers look elsewhere.

The 1980s car market is a prime example of this problem. Some U.S. car manufacturers mistakenly thought sacrificing quality in order to lower prices would lure customers. Initially it did. What they eventually learned was that lower prices and low quality was a losing proposition. Over time their customers migrated to higher quality, price competitive imports. U.S. car manufacturers lost significant market share and some companies needed an infusion of cash to stay afloat long enough to rectify the problem.

A product must balance quality and price.
It must be:
- Cost effective
- Desirable
- Somewhat Unique

Positive Energy:

Party Plan exists, due in large part, to its positive energy. Motivation keeps salespeople going. Excitement generates new business. Positive attitude keeps it going.

To maintain positive energy there must be:

- Sales meetings and/or training to create enthusiasm
- New products and catalogs at least 2x a year
- An exciting reward system that is attainable and desirable
- Positive thinking sales force
- Energy that draws you in

Programs:

There are usually 3 levels of incentive programs: Hostess, consultant, and manager.

Program incentives need to be:

- A reward that is enticing so people work for them
- Reasonable---If the goal is too high, people become defeated before they start
- Reasonable for the company so they are not spending too much on gifts

People:

Party Plan's foundation is its people. There are three groups of people that affect a party plan's success: 1. Management, 2. Sales force, and 3. Customers.

Each company needs

Management that is:

- Competent
- Knowledgeable
- Learns from mistakes
- Open to new ideas

Management needs to be aware of the mechanics in party plan sales. Party plan requires a unique mind set. A successful party plan has leaders with experience or advisors with plenty of party plan experience

Sales force that is:

- Varying ages and expertise
- Willing to share ideas
- Open and friendly

Customers who are:

- Satisfied with the product
- Willing to host or attend parties
- Fun!

Remember, it is always in the company's best interest to have you in their sales force but it may not be in your best interest. I am not saying that it is not a good idea to join the sales force of a new company or one that is undergoing a change. Realize what the potential risks are. Keep in mind the time invested in a company is time wasted if the company decides to call it quits.

Now you must decide what kind of consultant you would like to be. In party plan, you are the boss. You decide how to run your business, who you do business with, and how much time you devote to your business each week. You may start as one type of consultant and change to another as your knowledge, comfort level, and circumstances dictate.

All types of consultants have the potential for success. Each person's idea of success is different. For some it is paying off a large debt, others more financial freedom, other may want to take a crack at being their own boss and calling their own hours, while others may thrive on the acknowledgment of their peers. Whatever success is to you, it can be realized in party plan with the proper attitude and commitment.

Consultant Types

Career

The consultants in this group are looking for a full time job. They generally want to build their business by holding a minimum number or parties a week for a certain level of income. They are motivated and enjoy offering the opportunity to others. Usually they become managers or supervisors in a fairly short amount of time.

- ❖ Serious about the business & treats it as a job, not a hobby
- ❖ Willing to work for advancement
- ❖ Sees the "big picture"
- ❖ No immediate plans to leave the company

Double Duty

Consultants in this group are part time workers and spend fewer hours per week on their business. They need added income which may be steady or intermittent.

- ❖ Has another job but is committed to work a certain amount each week or month
- ❖ May be considering a career in party plan but needs to do Double duty with their other job until they are sure about the business
- ❖ May intend to keep their full time job and use party plan as extra money

Social Butterfly

- ❖ Is working more for fun than money
- ❖ Usually motivated by rewards and recognition
- ❖ Stop working if the fun stops
- ❖ Not extremely interested in advancing to management

Party Hopper
- ❖ Joins different party plan companies to get the merchandise and discounts
- ❖ Interested in free and discounted merchandise
- ❖ Does not commit to any party plan
- ❖ May eventually find one that fits his or her needs and style

Friends and Family
- ❖ Not interested in a career—usually has a full time job
- ❖ Sells to friends and family for the fun of getting together and a little extra money
- ❖ Does not try to find new customers or hostesses
- ❖ Usually does not do many parties and has minimal sales

Try It Again
- ❖ Repeat consultant
- ❖ Left for reasons that have now disappeared or been resolved
- ❖ Usually more committed to selling this time

There are over 18 million people in direct marketing/party plan. It is an ever growing, ever changing environment. Party plan motivates many people to achieve greater heights than most average jobs. There is a positive attitude that permeates through the entire company and a network of support and encouragement seldom found in other jobs. Every consultant has the opportunity for management if they so desire.

Party plan can be a long term commitment or a job that fills a need for a shorter time. No matter what your circumstances there is likely a type of consultant that fits your needs and lifestyle if you have the desire to explore this type of career path. Jump in and get your feet wet; you may find you love it!

CHAPTER 3
Preparation, Practice, Party!

Now that you made the decision to enter the world of party plan sales, your expectations are high and a positive attitude permeates your entire world. Everything is new and exciting. The early infancy of your business is a bit overwhelming and it is very unsteady. At this point it does not take much to encourage or discourage you. Proper training builds the foundation and persistence keeps you going. Do not let others rain on your parade. Party plan is a fun, rewarding career.

Many salespeople are brought into party plan with the phrase, "The product sells itself." No such product exists. Some sell much easier that others, but any business takes work to be successful. It is no different in party plan. Your success depends on the amount of time and effort you expend to launch and develop your new business. If you wait for business to come to you, you set yourself up to fail.

The first essential ingredient that helps ensure your success is training. The difference between success and failure depends heavily on how much support and training you receive during your first few of weeks of your new venture. Since this is your business, make it your business to experience any and all training available to you and maintain contact with your immediate supervisor. A well prepared consultant develops a profitable business.

Unfortunately, some salespeople have stories of being handed a kit and having to wing it. How sad that their manager did not take the time to train them adequately. Poor training in the beginning creates a stumbling block. If you are fortunate enough to have a manager with terrific training skills, take advantage of their knowledge and experience. It is your business and it is up to you to make sure you have the training you need. If your manager does not offer training or does an inadequate job, seek out training elsewhere. Ask other managers or consultants for assistance. The person who suffers the most from poor training is you.

Remember; you can never have too much training!!! Training is your solid base. Once you are properly trained, there is no limit to the income you can generate. Basic company training consists of paperwork, product knowledge, and company procedures. Personal training is acquired through your own party experience and the experiences of other consultants and managers.

Initially, your manager should be holding your hand until you feel confident to do things on your own. Ask for assistance and ideas. Be like sponge and absorb everything you can. If your manager/supervisor does not offer the chance to watch her work at a couple of her parties, this is the perfect time to ask to go with her. It is a great chance to take notes and see her style. If possible, go with another good consultant to add another style. You eventually develop your own way of doing a party. The more varied your training, the better rounded you are. You can even try different techniques to see which one works for your personality and customers.

Observe at least two parties with other consultants or your manager. Only so much information can be absorbed by reading manual or taking notes in a training meeting. Hands-on training is always the best. Things go wrong, consultants make mistakes. You learn more from the problems and how to solve them at actual parties than observing staged demonstrations for training purposes that are perfectly executed.

Most party plans have training meetings at regular intervals. This training provides a wealth of varied information and ideas from experienced salespeople in the company. Everything from how-to-do your business, to creative ideas for marketing, dating parties, recruiting, etc. A well-trained salesperson makes more money, has fewer problems, provides better customer service, and becomes a manager faster, than a poorly trained one.

Good training = More sales = Bigger paycheck

You have everything to gain by being properly trained and much to lose when you lack it. You may muddle through but it takes a lot longer for you to flourish. Remember time is money and every day you struggle is a day of pay lost that cannot be recaptured. Sometimes you have to be aggressive about receiving training. If you look around, you can find training. Do not wait for it to come looking for you!

Step 1: Ask for Parties

As you continue with your training, you also need to acquire your initial party line-up. Almost all companies require a minimum number of parties to establish the foundation of your business, usually five or six. This is your first on the job training skill. First, make a list of contacts for your initial parties. Even if you are not normally a person who makes lists, become one. Carry a notebook with you and when you think of names, jot them down. If you need 5 starter parties, list at least 20 or 30 names of people who might host one for you. The average percentage of yes answers is 20-25%.

Convincing 5-6 people that they would like to host a party for you is probably one of the most challenging duties you face. You are stepping out of your comfort zone to ask for your initial parties. For most people this is very difficult. Even people who have been in another party plan sometimes find this arduous but it is the heart of your business. Without parties, there is no party plan business.

Persistence does pay off. If you ask everyone you know, at least 5 want to help you or at the very least feel sorry enough for you to host one. Most people want to help a friend or family member succeed.

Try this 3 step method when talking to friends and family:

Start by saying,

"I've started my own business"

Give a 30 second synopsis on your business

And quickly follow-up with

"I need your help."

Then immediately ask for what you want!
"Could you invite a few friends over so I can practice my demonstration?"

     You asked them to help you in your new venture by hosting a party; now assure them that it does not matter how many guests attend. It is more important that you practice your presentation. Once the worry of not hosting a successful party for you is dispelled, your friends and relatives are more likely to agree to host a party. They want you to succeed. If all you are concerned about at this point is learning and practicing, they know they can easily help you do that.

     The trick to perpetuating the party chains beyond your initial parties is to try to schedule as many different groups of people as possible. If Mom, Sue, sister Shelley, cousin Alice, and Aunt Jane are at all 5 of your first parties, the party possibilities are very limited. You need different groups of friends, and family in order to increase your variety of party chains. You do not want to have to start over again after your initial parties are completed. Nor do you want all your friends and relatives to have a closet full of the product you are selling to help you out. You are starting a new venture to make money, not depend the people closest to you to keep you in business.

     Once you have your first parties scheduled, you have successfully completed the first challenging hurdle of this business. Even though you have the required amount of parties, the search for more parties is not finished. Carry your business wherever you go. Show your excitement and enthusiasm for your new venture. Excitement is contagious. Talk, talk, talk. Let everyone you come in contact with know what you are doing. Search for more parties everywhere you go.

     Prepare hostess packets. The faster you get these packets to your starter party hostess, the less chance of cancellation and the more time she has to collect outside orders. Purchase an inexpensive stamp with at least your name and phone number on it; website if possible. It is one of the easiest ways to advertise your business. Everything that is in the packet should be stamped with your contact information. Get in the habit of keeping packets prepared and ready to give to hostesses.

You now have 5 or 6 parties and prepared hostess packets, you must now coach your hostesses. Even if the people who agreed to host a party have had one before, coach them anyway. You need practice and they may not know how your party plan is run, what they offer, or it may have been awhile and they need a refresher course on hosting a successful party. They certainly never hosted a party with you.

Step 2: Hostess coaching

All hostesses need to be coached. Hostess coaching is the difference between a good party and a great one. Always keep in mind that your hostess cleans and prepares her home for guests, shops for or cooks refreshments, and then sends her husband, boyfriend, kids, or other distractions out the door for a few hours. This is no minor task. When a person agrees to host a party, those are the tasks she knows she must accomplish. In order for her to agree, she must accept the extra work. By hostess coaching, you are helping her earn compensation for her time and effort. If you do not hostess coach or do a poor job of it, it is a grave disservice to her.

A hostess should not be a onetime shot. You want her to think, "Wow! Look at all the free product. That was easy!" Your goal is to create the desire for a repeat performance. How do you do this? By teaching your hostess how to do it. Do not assume she remembers the steps even if she hosted a party for you in the past. Everyone benefits from a refresher course. There should be very little difference between the time you spend with a new hostess and a repeat one. Every hostess deserves your time. Spending time with a hostess tells her you care and that you do not take her for granted. If you hand a repeat hostess a packet and say, "You remember what to do, right?" She will say, "Yes" even if she is not sure. Usually, both of you suffer and sales reflect the amount of time the two of you devoted to this party.

Set the bar high. Shoot for a $500 party. Talk $500 parties. Expect $500 parties. When you practice always referring to this level of sales, slowly your party average rises. People rise to the level of expectation you present to them. Of course, every party cannot be a $500 party but it should always be the goal and like any other goal, sometimes you reach it and sometimes you do not. But, when you stretch your sights, you ALWAYS attain a higher level than without a goal. The same is true for your hostess. Give her a goal and show her how to go for it!

Go over every piece of paper in the packet. Some items need more explanation than others. Reiterate the time and date of the party and make sure it is a workable date for her. If there is any question about the chosen day, reschedule it. Better to do it now than to receive a phone call a day or two before the party when it is too late to date another party in that slot. It is perfectly fine to enlighten her on the workings of a party plan datebook. Explain to her that you are keeping this date exclusively for her and you work a certain number of days. You fill your datebook accordingly and when parties cancel, it affects you. I always told them, "This is my job and I only get paid if I work. So we need to make sure this date still works for you. Of course, sometimes there are circumstances beyond our control but as far as you know, is this still a great time for you and your friends?" This creates accountability and responsibility. I let her know I understand uncontrollable events but make sure she is committed to follow through with the party.

Inform her the best time to send our invitations, email or social media is 7-8 days before the party. Too far ahead people forget; too close to the party and plans are already made.

Pull out a catalog and turn to the page that displays the hostess program. You can explain how to read the chart. Later, the hostess can refresh her memory and chart her progress herself--- a self motivated hostess always sells more merchandise! Never refer to the lowest qualifying level. Remember the rule for hostess coaching—think $500 party and 3 parties. Show her how much she receives free at this level. When she earns above average product, you earn an above average paycheck.

The hostess must write down her wish list. No matter what goal a person is reaching for, the key is to solidify the goal by writing it down. Tell her to dream big and write down all the products she loves. If she picks out a small item, this is a signal to you. You need to expand her expectations. You can say, "No, I mean a real dream item!" Give her the catalog and request she look again and think big.

Now, show her how to earn it! Go to the catalog and locate the amount on the chart but do not just use the sales chart. The lifeblood of your business is parties so always, always talk sales and parties. If the item she picked out is not at the $500 and 3 level then you say, "Okay, what else?" Continue this until she reaches that level. Most hostesses are amazed at the amount of free merchandise possible.

You are stretching, challenging, and educating your hostess. She is excited and her party reflects the enthusiasm you nurtured. If you make 30% commission, the difference between a $300 party and a $500 is $60. If you are holding 4 parties a week that could mean up to $240 a month or $2900 a year difference in your paycheck. The same amount of work and time, just more paycheck.

Finally, I reiterate to the hostess the importance of contacting everyone 1-2 days before the party. This is the #1 reason parties succeed or fail! When guests are not contacted by the hostess, the odds of a successful party dramatically decrease. Remind **every** hostess to call 1 or 2 days ahead even if they are a repeat hostess. I always told my hostesses, "Your attendance is higher and of course, your sales, too, if you call and remind your guests. You may think you are pestering them, but people are busy and sometimes just plain forget. If you feel uncomfortable doing the calls, blame me. Tell your guests I need to know how many guests you are expecting."

Call (not text) her the day before she should have sent out invites to find out if she has done her inviting, how she is doing on her outside orders, and if she has encountered anyone who would like to host their own party. This call keeps continued contact with your hostess and jogs her memory about inviting her friends and family if she hasn't done it already.

When you call her 1-2 days before the party to see how she is doing and ask her how many she is expecting at this point. This is a good time to make sure she is making her reminder calls. If she has not done it yet, gently remind her that she has the best turnout if she calls to remind her guests about her party. Never assume a party is still happening without a confirmation from the hostess a day or two prior to the date.

Make sure you and your hostess have contact a minimum of 3 times— at hostess coaching, a week before the party and a couple of days prior to the party to see how everything is progressing. Some of these can be texts but at least one should be phone contact. One of the most frustrating things is for your first party to reschedule after all that preparation. The more contact you maintain with your hostess, the less chance there is of rescheduling unless the hostess has an unexpected issue.

Step 3: Getting Ready

At this point, you should have your kit. If you haven't already, take it out of the box! Set it up as you would at a party and practice, practice, practice. The more comfortable you are with the merchandise, the better your demonstration. Buy some blank stickers and write the name of the item, page it appears in the catalog, and price. You can tell the guests it is for their convenience but it is actually your cheat sheet. The guests at my parties expected the merchandise to be tagged with this information, so I always had it marked. If you have merchandise that changes frequently, this is great way to appear very knowledgeable and customer oriented. The customers perceive this as a service you do for them.

Even if you are very familiar with the product you have chosen to sell, demonstrating it is a whole different prospective. What does it do? What is its use? Could it have more than one use so you can market it better? You don't need to memorize every piece but your first party is not the place to start looking at the product information manual. Read through the manual that accompanies it so you are familiar with many of the items in your kit.

Your first party is getting closer and you need to practice and get ready to do a good demonstration. Before you arrive at the first party, you should have practiced what you are going to do and say multiple times. Set up your display with some décor and demonstrate the merchandise to your husband, kids, or close friends. This helps you understand where you need improvement and become comfortable with the merchandise you are selling.

Step 4: The Party

Think of the word party. You associate fun and laughter with it. Well, the first word in party plan is party. If you are not having fun, than you are in the wrong business. A great side benefit to party plan is the fun. You can forget to bring merchandise, prizes, or even catalogs and everyone can still have a wonderful night. Hostesses have parties to get their friends together and have fun. If your demonstration goes perfectly, that is good but it is definitely not a necessary ingredient for success.

Every consultant has stories about embarrassing parties. They usually are still selling product. They can even laugh about it---most of the time. If you and your guests are having fun, you can forge ahead without almost anything. Consultants have forgotten supplies such as catalogs, order forms, game gifts, a date book, or even parts of their display. They just improvise and have a sense of humor.

Look professional and dress for success. When you make your first contact with a guest at the party, she has already decided whether she likes the way you look. This influences whether she hosts a party, becomes a consultant, or even places an order with you. Business casual is usually a safe choice. A big smile and a welcoming demeanor is a necessity. Wear your nametag and any buttons, pins, or awards you may have. People like to do business with successful people.

Décor helps create a festive, fun spirit. Try to have some kind of lighting or candles in your display. It is amazing how much more impressive a display you have with candles/ lighting. At holiday time, decorate your table with lights and holiday decorations. Even a small amount of holiday décor adds some festivity and variation to the table. Elevate parts of your display so the guests can see everything from their seat. Make sure your specials, both hostess and guest, stand out. An enticing display draws the guest's interest.

Another fun thing to do to add to the theme of your display is to dress according to the type of party you are holding. If you are doing a luau party, wear a dress or shirt with Hawaiian print. Dress for the seasons as well. Even if you do not own holiday attire, wear things like red or green for Christmas, harvest colors for fall, and pastels for the spring. Even a decorative pin, earrings, or scarf works. It helps everyone get into the spirit of the party and the guests love it.

Always arrive 30-45 minutes ahead of time so you have adequate time to set up your display and mingle with the arriving guests. If you rush through the door with only 10 or 15 minutes to set up the display, the party never feels relaxed. From the minute you arrive, it is your job to create a party atmosphere. The hostess invited the guests, collected orders, and prepared food. Now you need to finish the job and make her party a success.

When you enter her home, compliment her home, her animals, her outfit, etc. You want to make her feel special. She is very special to you. She is the backbone of your business. Without her, you would have no business. If you have time after you have set up the display, offer assistance and visit with her before the guests arrive.

As the guests start to arrive, offer to answer the door for her. This way she can finish what she is doing and you have a chance for initial contact with each guest. Welcome them and establish a connection. Find out where they work, where they are from, do they have children or grandchildren, etc. Parties are about creating relationships and connecting with people. Get to know as many guests as you can on a personal level. Many of these people become your party family. You want to become their personal consultant.

Once you begin your demonstration, thank your hostess. She is the star of the evening and should be made to feel special. Refer to her several times during the demonstration. Romance your product. If you can suggest a unique use, you usually sell a lot more of that particular product. Your job is to create a desire for the products you carry. Sometimes you entice a guest to purchase a product they wouldn't normally consider.

Invite the guests to think about upcoming occasions. Find out how many of them have ever rushed to the store at the last minute for a gift only to pay too much for an item, not exactly what they had in mind. Ask them if they have heard of an "In Case" closet or box. This is a collection of a few items in case you need a last minute gift. It saves time and money.

Throughout the demonstration encourage interaction with your merchandise. Pass certain items around the room. This also relaxes the guests about touching your display. If you have set up a beautiful display, many people are reluctant to disturb anything especially if it contains breakable items. When you dismantle it first, they tend to follow your lead. Sales significantly improve when the guests handle and touch the merchandise.

In addition to knowing the product, you also need to know your programs. Each party plan is different so you need to realize what your company offers. If you have specials for the guests, incentives for the hostess, and hostess free programs, it is important you know the basics of each program. People need to be told several times about the specials before they may remember them. Repeat. Repeat. Repeat. You want to entice people to become a hostess for you. The more you understand your programs and specials the more confidence you convey.

Step 5: Guest Relations

After you finish your demonstration, let them table shop and talk with each other. Let them talk amongst themselves and browse the merchandise. If you have encouraged them to touch the product, they should feel comfortable to approach the display table and handle the items. If not, walk back and reinforce that you want them to pick things up to see and feel them up close and personal.

Set up your office for helping guests total their orders separate from the hub of activity but close enough to politely hear their conversations. If you are able to hear them, they can ask you a question and you can respond. From close proximity you can hear key phrases like "I want ... but I can't afford it" so you can offer the opportunity to host a party of their own.

Remember, the #1 place to find parties is at the party. Your guests can see the merchandise; they are excited and having fun; they want to help their friend. A good demonstration creates the desire for more. The guests want a repeat performance. They want to attend another one or host a party themselves. Your primary focus is dating parties to help the hostess earn more free merchandise, perpetuate your party line-up, and expand your customer base.

If the guest refuses the opportunity to host her own party, offer alternative ways to connect with her. If she doesn't want to host her own party, offer the option of collecting orders and still earning free merchandise. If that does not appeal to her, ask if she wants to be on your contact list for upcoming events such as bingo or theme parties. Usually something peaks their interest. If at all possible, you do not want to lose touch with them.

Step 6: Rewarding your Hostess

After you finish with the orders and date as many parties as you can, let your hostess know the results of her efforts. Even if the party has been less than desirable, your job is to make her feel good about the party. I always let this hostess know that the bottom line is sales not attendance and lots of hostesses have had times when people for various reasons could not attend the party. That does not mean they don't want to order. Usually, websites are part of your business and people can get online and add an order.

If she has had a good party, this is the time to praise her efforts. I tell her how much I enjoyed her friends and family. I give examples of guests that I especially liked. Next, you let her know the actual amount of her sales, which guests have paid already, and how many parties she has acquired. This is to let her know where she is at that point so you can show her what is possible.

Always project her to the next level with either sales, parties, or both. You could say, "You are only $75 away from the next level where you can receive .... more in free merchandise. Do you have more people you need to show the catalog to?" Another question to ask is, "Is there anyone who didn't attend who you think might want to host her own party? An additional party would result in......more in free merchandise."

This increases your paycheck. It may not seem like much on one party, but it can add up quickly. Imagine you average $75 in additional sales per party. If you are holding 4 parties per week and make 30% commission, this means $90 more per week, $360 a month and $4680 a YEAR! It takes only a few more minutes to incentivize your hostess to want more free merchandise.

It is always better to close the party in person. The more personal contacts you have with your hostess, the better your relationship with her. Remember, you are selling yourself as well as your product. This is another time to talk with her about her party. There are two objectives. The first is to offer the opportunity to join your company. With most party plans, you can convert the party over to an introductory party and apply a percentage towards the kit. The second is to offer her the opportunity to rebook herself if she is not interested in joining the company. She usually earns even more merchandise for doing this.

Step 7: Paperwork

You have made it through your first party and closed it. Congratulations!
Just as in any other job; it is not complete until the paperwork is done. Ideally, a manager or very knowledgeable consultant should help you submit the first 2 or 3 orders. Online submission has made hostess orders much easier. Once you master all the necessary paperwork, it should be the least time consuming job you need to do. The trick is to keep it up to date and not let it pile up. When you complete the forms in a timely manner, it takes minutes not hours.

Step 8 Never Stop Learning

There are unlimited sources for obtaining advanced training. Generally, your company offers classes. Training outside your company is another great way to stretch your horizons. The more varied your training, the more rounded you are. Innovative and forward thinking individuals prosper more than stagnant, outdated ones.

Continued training is the proactive approach to your business. It makes you better equipped to handle the ups and downs of your sales career. When you are prepared, you are primed to weather almost any problems that arise. You need positive re-enforcement and training. Conversely, if all your parties are a huge success with high sales and plenty of bookings, you do not learn how to weather the rough spots. No matter whether you fizzle or sizzle, you need training.

Success is not the same for everyone. What one person may feel is a great success is barely adequate in another's eyes. One thing is for sure, a successful consultant is respected and in demand. Success happens when work meets preparation.

Here is an example of the form that is included in the Hostess packet:

Party Planner

Congratulations_____
> I am SO excited to have you as a HOSTESS!!!
> I know you and your friends will have fun at your party.

I have reserved this day and time for you:
> Date_____
> Time_____

We will be doing the Auction Party (if you are an in-home party)
> You receive $500 for 5 outside orders
> You receive $500 when you call and remind your guests
> You receive $500 for every person who has decided to have
> > a Party of their own BEFORE I get there.

> Guests receive $200 for every uninvited guest they
> > bring with them

3 SIMPLE RULES FOR SUCCESS!!
> 1.) Invitations 7 days before the party date.
> 2.) Take your catalogs everywhere—collect orders from
> > people who cannot attend.
> 3.) CONTACT everyone 1-2 days before the party to
> > remind them.

> > *****Remember 10-5-1*****
> > 10 Guests in Attendance
> > 5 Outside Orders—in person or on the website
> > Have 1 Booking waiting for me

Any questions do not hesitate to call me. I will be in touch with you.
Thanks again for dating a party with me.

(Your name and phone number)

Chapter 4
Parties are Everywhere

In this chapter, we look at the various ways to find parties. Do you have a party today? If not, you should use the time to make contacts. If you do not contact people, you cannot generate new parties. Parties are virtually everywhere. The key is to ask the people you meet. If you use a wide variety of the ways listed in this chapter to find parties, your date book is full, and you are making great money, and gain more confidence. As always, the best place to date parties are at your parties but the purpose of this chapter is to assist you in finding parties in other ways as well. Sometimes you discover an unexpected, interesting avenue to find new party chains. Make a habit of stepping out of your comfort zone every day.

Ideally, your parties should generate enough parties to sustain your business. If each party resulted in 2-3 more parties, you would be very successful. Unfortunately, some parties are dead ends with no additional parties added to your datebook. A string of bad luck can force a number of parties to cancel. The weather can force cancellations. No matter what the reasons, you need skills to find more parties and keep your business going strong.

When you are dating parties, here is an easy way to remember what to do:

D – Determination -- Do not give up

A -- Attitude -- it is not what you say but how you say it

T – Thank you –write it and say it often

I – Incentivize –make it worth everyone's time and effort

N – New Products & Promotions—create excitement over your product

G – Goals!—sales, long term, short term, parties........Always have a goal

Making Calls

One of the most essential skills to develop is phone calling. It is a very important skill. The phone is your #1 tool in party plan. You need to use it daily. It is the most economical and fastest way to reach a prospective hostess. Phone calling is a great way to date parties from leads at a party, referrals, or customer service follow-ups. The key is to call consistently. Set a goal to make at least 5 calls a day and you WILL be successful. It is a game of numbers. The more people you contact, the greater the success rate.

Every time you pick up the phone and talk to someone, you are getting closer to a yes. Rejection is part of the sales game. You need to develop the ability to roll with the punches and not take it personally. Most salespeople believe you have to reach a certain NO quota before you get a yes. If you hear 10-15 NO's before you receive a YES, this is a high success rate. Each person has to find their own individual success average. Find out what your success rate is so you can adjust the needed amount of calls.

Many people try to avoid the phone by sending out flyers, new hostess specials etc either by email blasts, websites, and/or social media postings thinking it generates calls for parties. This rarely happens. What actually happens is you spend tremendous amounts of time and energy with little or no return for your investment. There are thousands of logo pens, business cards and other advertising materials for various companies. This type of bonus advertising without follow-up calls is virtually useless. At least 75% of your success is either face to face or over the phone contact with potential hostesses telling them about your product. If you do choose this avenue for finding new parties, always do the follow-up calling for the personal contact. This dramatically improves the amount of parties you book with these sales tools.

Never stop calling. Seek out new business every day----every single day! A big mistake many salespeople make is to stop calling when they are at their busiest. In party sales, you need to think and date parties, three weeks ahead. When you look at your date book and have empty days anytime in those three weeks—

CALL! It is twice the work to get back to where you were than to maintain your party schedule.

Here are a few rules for a successful phone calling session:
1.) Set a specific amount of time to make calls and stick to it.
2.) Make your phone calls in your office or a secluded area so you are not interrupted during your call session.
3.) Have the calls you are going to make written down
    Take notes on each call for reference later.
4.) Dress for Success–even though you are on the phone and the person at the other end of the line can't see you, you have a better self image if you are nicely dressed.
5.) Project a positive attitude--people respond in kind
6.) Have the script you have practiced (not memorized) and any information handy that you need to tell the person at the other end--specials, new products, etc. Pictures or catalogs
7.) Listen!!!!.
8.) KISS—keep it short and simple
9.) Ask for the commitment.
10.) End every call on a positive note. **Thank** them for their time whether they dated a party or not

Let's get CALLING!
First, brainstorm and make a list of everyone you know. Your ultimate goal is to call different groups of people. You do not want to work in the same circle of people all the time. That decreases your party average and eventually you reach a dead end and have to start all over again.
Divide your prospects into A, B, & C groups. The A group contains people you feel comfortable calling and are the most likely to say YES. People on the B list are a little more difficult. The C lists are mostly referrals and follow up calls. Usually, you are not very comfortable calling these people and they are challenging. Decide which category each person falls into, write them down and list them under their corresponding groups.

Even before you even pick up the phone, you must be ready. This means you need to know what you are offering the hostess and why she should do it. I use a short script. There is a difference between a canned script and a rehearsed one. When you rehearse your script, it sounds more natural the more you practice and use it. Just as an actor or actress rehearses their script until it appears natural, you need to do the same thing. Your script should vary from person to person. Customizing your speech is necessary! But if you lose your train of thought, hesitate or use filler words (you know, and, um), your effectiveness is lost. Do not memorize it. For the most part, it should be natural conversation. Practice the key points so you do not forget them.

Your opening statement sets the tone for the entire phone call. If you feel hesitant, it translates into your voice and the person at the other end responds accordingly---usually with a no. If you just finished yelling at your kids or arguing with your husband, your tone indicates irritation. I am not advocating NOT making calls, instead, adjust your attitude and tone of voice. Call a friendly hostess or another consultant. Do whatever is necessary to readjust your attitude and mood.

Since the hardest part of phone calling is actually picking up the phone, I make my first call a "YES". This is a call to a person who just needs to pick a date for her party or a hostess to find out how she is doing on her party. You need to create a positive tone for your calling. Make it a short call. You do not want to waste precious time with social chitchat. Progress as quickly as possible to the next call. If you still need a confidence booster, call another "A" list potential hostess.

Here is an example of how a conversation should progress:

1.) Introduce yourself with the name of your Party Plan and say: "Is this a good time for you?" If yes, continue. If no, find out a better time to call back. Always ask her if it is a good time to talk. There is nothing more counterproductive than assuming it is okay to start talking and get halfway through your talk when the person at the other end cuts you off. Now she is even more irritated and has a negative attitude. Even if she agrees to listen to you, be aware of subtle clues that it is a less than perfect time for her to talk.

If you sense a potentially negative situation, address it. You can say, "It sounds like this is a bad time for you. Would you like me to call back at a better time?" They appreciate the easy out you have just provided for them. You have also kept a potentially valuable contact. If you had pushed on, you may have lost the contact permanently

Here are some clues to the situation the other end of the phone
- *The person answers in an irritated or rushed tone*
- *Loud background noise---party or lots of company*
- *Screaming children or baby*
- *Mate asking—"Who is calling?!"*
- *Voice that sounds sickly*

2.) Ask questions and share information; carry on a friendly conversation. Once she has given you the okay to begin, ask questions about her and find out about her life. This business is about building relationships. You need to know about your hostess and she needs to know you. Share information and comment accordingly. If you already have a relationship with this hostess, this is where you reconnect and catch up on her life. Use your best listening skills.

3.) Resume with the purpose of the call. "The reason I am calling you today is to let you know that we have …(wonderful new merchandise or specials. Describe them and create the desire)." Explain why she should host a party and how she can benefit. Make it so attractive that she has a hard time saying no. Know what you are offering. I keep a current catalog in front of me and a list of the hostess specials. There is nothing worse than losing your train of thought and not being able to remember what

you are offering. It is not very professional and sometimes it is the difference between a party and losing one
Elaborate extensively!

4.) Listen Again. After you give her your information, listen to her response. It is very important for you to let her voice her opinion and/or objection. The only way you are able to overcome her objections is to know them. Do not talk fast. Getting all the information to her faster does not guarantee a positive response from her. If you dominate the conversation, the person at the other end of the phone tunes out. A conversation should be two sided. By allowing your potential hostess to respond, it quickly becomes a friendly banter. You do not want the person to move into the defense mode; also known as the NO mode.

5.) Close the deal. Once you have finished describing the offer, immediately go to the closing. "I would like to set a date for us to get together with some of your friends and family so you can see our great merchandise and receive free merchandise too. I have Tuesday the 16th or Thursday the 18th available." Stop; listen to the answer and respond accordingly.

The closing is very much about timing and intuition. There is no formula for a guaranteed yes, but if you do not close your presentation, it is a guaranteed waste of time. Once you established a relationship, you need to ask for the party. You are calling to set dates for parties. The person on the other end of the phone knows the purpose of your call. Do not waste her time and yours by beating around the bush. By avoiding your purpose, you are prolonging the answer. Just ask!

Keep in mind the first no is not necessarily a permanent no. The person you are talking to usually gives you hints about why they do not want to host a party. Your job is to listen to the objection and try to overcome it. Assess why they object to hosting a party. Maybe they have had a bad experience with a party before. On the other hand, maybe they are afraid no one will show up to their party. Listen and decide how to resolve her objections. Ideally, you convince her to host a party. If you cannot ally her objections, ask permission to keep her on a customer update list for future calling. Do not lose the connection you established.

The approach is a little different for the B and C groups. You may have to ask if she remembers you from wherever the contact with her originated. Definitely more time is spent on the friendly conversation banter. The biggest difference is the transition from conversation to asking for the party. This takes some practice. Keep practicing! Sometimes you call at a bad time. Ask her when she would like you to call back—what would be a better time? If she tells you June, make sure you call her then–not July or August. Have a notebook where you can record notes about your conversation. This is vital information for follow-up call later. You cannot possibly remember everything about everyone.

Overcoming Objections

The first thing you must understand is why your hostess has a party. There are a few main reasons; to earn free merchandise; an excuse to get her friends together; to help support a friend in her new endeavor or to help her friend receive free merchandise from her party. Your job is to create excitement for any of these reasons. When you are trying to overcome an objection and encourage someone to become a hostess, you need to find out what reason entices her most.

Remember, the person at the other end of the phone needs your understanding. Success rate increases as you learn to say the right thing at the right time. With practice, you are able to address and overcome most objections. Anytime you can personalize your response, it helps the person you are talking to know you really understand their situation. Association gives credence to your responses. The more experiences you have in life, the easier it becomes to overcome objections. Honestly talk to people. No one can handle all objections or experience every situation but empathizing can turn resistance into a party.

Here are some sample objections and responses:

I'm too Busy!

Whether a stay at home mom or a person who works outside the home, people are busy.

First acknowledge their challenge, "I understand how busy you are!

*** How about if I drop over with a few of our new items? You could invite a couple of friends over so they can see the merchandise in person. I'll give you a free gift just for inviting some friends to your house."

OR

*** Does your office or job ever allow lunch hour or after work parties? I can bring a limited amount of merchandise and give you free merchandise for hosting it.

I don't know enough people

Most people think that they need to have many people for a successful party. An average party is 4-6 people. Usually they are amazed to find out the average attendance is so small.

You can also prompt them by asking if they attend church, are involved in sports, clubs, kids activities, co-workers, etc. Once you get them to relax and think about how many people they actually know and come in contact with on a regular basis, they are usually surprised. Before long, the list is quite adequate.

My friends have all been to a lot of parties lately

Suggest you book a tentative date a month out so her friends have a chance to recuperate. "That would work, wouldn't it?" This is what I like to call the statement/question. It is meant to be more of a statement than a question. It needs an answer but if the person has a strong objection to what I have just proposed, the opening is there.

I don't do parties!

Find out if she had a bad experience. If she did, you can alleviate
her fears about your company by giving some testimonials.
Sometimes you can even correct her problem. I called a guest to
try to date a party with her and she proceeded to tell me how she
hated my company. In talking with her I realized she had a small
defective part that was never returned to her. It cost me $1.59!!! I
replaced it for her. She did not have a party but she gave me some
leads that developed into great party chains.

If she did not have a bad experience, find out why she doesn't want
to have a party and overcome it if possible. Many of these
objections and solutions can be conquered.

I don't want to clean my house

Promote holding a party at the local pizza place. This is a great
alternative to hosting a party in their home. They do not need to
prepare refreshments because they serve pizza and soda. No
cleaning and there is a lot more room. In addition, you can offer
the opportunity of pairing up with a friend or sister and having a
double party.

I don't have enough room to host a party

I have talked to people who lived in 2500 sq. ft. homes that
thought they had small rooms. Some people certainly do live in
cramped quarters. However, I think they would have to tell me
they lived in a closet before I would have to concede they
definitely did not have the room after the experience I had with a
young hostess of mine.

*A young potential hostess told me she lived in a very small
apartment. I told her I would bring less merchandise and set it up
around her apartment. She agreed and became very excited at the
prospect of hosting her first home party. She definitely did her job*

as a hostess. She collected outside orders, made light refreshments, over-invited, and called all of her guests to invite them personally.

I walked in the night of the party and barely found a place to set my merchandise. It was VERY small. The living room and bedroom were one and the same. The kitchen could hold 3 people. She apologized profusely for the size of the apartment but I reassured her it would be fine even though I had grave doubts.

I set up a small display by the T.V. and put things various places around the room. I used every available flat area on furniture and shelves. Then the guests started to arrive. Ten people walked through the door. I could not imagine where they would fit.

People shared chairs, sat on the bed, or whatever floor space was available. Others stood in the kitchen peaking in. They did not seem to mind how many people had to move just to let someone through to the bathroom. The demonstration and auction generated more and more excitement. No one seemed to mind the cramped space or the limited amount of merchandise.

Everyone had a blast. I don't think I ever had a party where there was so much giggling and laughing. The refreshments were served with everyone's assistance. A sense of genuine camaraderie prevailed. Just like the structure you live in does not guarantee a happy home, lots of space does not mean a successful party. People make the difference not houses or apartments.

When trying to convince someone their home would be fine, I tell them the story of the efficiency apartment and they usually laugh and say, "Well, I have more room than that!"

We all would like to think that as great salespeople we can overcome any objection. The reality is we cannot. Some people never host a party no matter what you offer them for whatever reason. The key is to know when to stop trying to overcome their objection and offer an alternative.

Referrals and Follow-Up Calls

Everyone cannot be a hostess. We need guests to attend these parties too. You need to remember this when you are talking to people. Find her need and fill it. This may not be hosting a party. Most people are very glad to give you referrals. They want to help you but cannot or will not have a party and they feel this is a way to do it. It is never a wasted contact if you come away with something positive. You could receive a referral that decides to host a fantastic party for you or even become a consultant and sell the plan. The key is to ASK!

You can ask several questions. "If someone in your neighborhood (or someone you know) had a party would you like to be invited?" "Do you know anyone who likes to give parties?" "Would you be interested in collecting a few orders?" Most people who do not host parties, attend them. Keep these people in your database especially when new merchandise is introduced. Even if they don't attend a party, they may give you a sizeable order. Remember that these people never host parties so these extra orders are bonus income.

Salespeople lose thousands of dollars every year because they neglect follow-up calls. Follow-up calls are customer service calls. You already invested time with the initial contact. If you do not reconnect with this person, you have wasted that time. Multiply this by the number of follow-up calls you do not complete, it can actually be tremendous amounts of time and money. You can lose customers when you do not complete them in a timely manner.

When people tell you to call later, the perception is they are telling you that in order to get you off their back. Of course, in some cases this is true. Unfortunately, when you assume this is the case, you are losing potential sales and contacts. Before I learned the importance of calling when you agree to call, I let many leads grow cold. I thought if they were still on my list, they were a yes just waiting for me to call. Nothing could be farther from the truth. Whenever you told them you were going to call—do it!

I met Cheryl at one of my parties in February. I immediately loved her enthusiasm and easy manner with other guests. She seemed to enjoy meeting the guests she did not know. They, in turn, seemed to gravitate toward her. I knew I wanted to ask her to join my team. She possessed so many of the qualities that are found in successful consultants. Her personality lit up the room, people felt comfortable approaching her, and she did not hesitate to interact with people she did not know.

The first step for consultants is with an initial party so I popped the question as she finished her order. "How about inviting a few friends over?" She informed me of her other commitments for the next 2 months but said she would like to have a party later. She told me to call in April and she would host a party for me. Disappointed, but hopeful, I wrote her name in my book under April and smugly thought I could easily recruit her when she finally did host a party.

I needed to call her in mid-March to book the party. April arrived and I continued to procrastinate. I kept moving her name to the next list of people I needed to call. In my mind, if I did not call, I had a yes waiting for confirmation. She attended a party for another competitor and that consultant did not hesitate to invite her to join their company.

I finally called in May. When I talked to her, she informed me she had an introductory party the following week with another company. Not only did I lose a party, I lost a .possible consultant for my company. A costly lesson in "do it now!" Most sales and recruit opportunities are timing. If I called her in April, there is a good chance she'd be working at my party plan instead of a competitors.

Sometimes, the follow up time is five or six months out. These people should not be left to grow cold. How do you call these people especially if they expressed the desire to wait quite awhile? One way is to call and say, "I was thinking about you the other day so I decided to give you a call." If you know what she likes or collects you could add, "The Company just came out with a new collection of frogs and I knew you'd love to see them."

Even if you do not date a party, you maintained contact with her. She knows you have taken an interest in her and your name stays in her mind.

Turning outside orders into parties

If a customer calls and places a large order, call her and say, "Do you know you are missing out on a great opportunity?" This peaks her curiosity and invariably she asks, "What great opportunity?" Explain that with just little more in sales, she can qualify to get free merchandise. Relay that you would be happy to just place your order and make more profit, but would love to give her some free merchandise. Propose that you order her merchandise and when you deliver it to her she can invite a few friends and they can see a few new items---no demonstration, just coffee. Would that work?

Most people want to see new merchandise and a get-together is less intimidating than a party. She already ordered and obviously likes the merchandise. Chances are her friends might want some of your merchandise once they see it in person. This is creative marketing. Some large parties generate very few leads. And sometimes a small party generates a party or a consultant lead for each guest in attendance. You can never judge a situation. Take advantage of every opportunity for a new party. When you find new hostesses and guests, it is a new opportunity to book new chains of parties and recruit new consultants into your business.

The phone is your #1 tool but it is not your only tool. There are other avenues to book parties. Developing new chains of parties require innovation and stepping out of the box. The following ways to book parties definitely stretcj your boundaries. Try them all and find what works best for you. You may find an exhilarating new way to acquire parties

Events and Fairs

Working a fair or event is another very good way to date parties into very different circles. Diversity is one of the key factors for becoming and staying successful in party plan. What you must realize before you even decide to do a fair is they are a lot of HARD work and you may have to do a few before you realize a difference in your party line-up. Sometimes you have to be patient and persistent in order to see the results. The results are not always immediate, but no one who works fairs consistently is wanting for different circles of parties. It is a natural development of fairs and events. You are reaching sometimes thousands of new potential hostesses and customers. The secret is in the planning, execution, and follow-up of the event.

Find out when and where these events take place. There are several resources for finding them—the local chamber of commerce, calling schools (which may have less costly fairs), and surfing the internet. In scheduling these events, keep in mind the areas you would like to work. Remember, this is where many of the parties occur. If you are 2 hours away from your home, you may want to reconsider. I highly recommend doing no more than one event or fair a month. It takes time to do a successful event and you need time to hold your parties as well.

The execution of the event is crucial to your success. This is where you book your parties, generate leads, and find new customers. "You can't meet from your seat". This means literally NO SITTING! Most people are not going to enter your booth to enter the drawing and fill out the form. Create a fair special to entice people to date parties with you. Talk with people as they walk by your booth. Create a booth that lures people to come look at what you have to offer. One of the best ways is too add lighting and movement especially things that sing and dance!

Have at least one other person working the booth with you. If you are busy, two people are the minimum that can handle a booth. There is nothing worse than talking with a person, almost ready to set a date for her party when another customer interrupts to ask a question about a product. Sometimes this break in momentum can lose you the party. There are two goals when working a fair; to date parties immediately and to generate leads from the drawing slips for more potential parties.

The planning was great; the execution smooth and productive, but the true measure of the success of a fair is the follow-up. In reality, the only people you put into your date book are the ones who are excited about the product they see or are enticed by the extra free merchandise for actually dating a party at the fair. There are MANY more parties in those drawing slips!

Sometimes a fair seems to be a total failure. While it may seem like a waste of time if you did not get many parties at your event, leads can be generated with drawing forms that were filled out. If you call the leads, parties are generated from a fair for many months. Calling leads from the drawing slips makes a difference. The success or failure of a fair is in your hands.

The amount of places and ideas of where to get parties is infinite. The key is to think outside the box, be creative, and always be looking for a potential hostess wherever you go. The more different avenues you use to get parties, the more varied your circle of guests and the more parties are potentially at your fingertips. The sky is the limit!

15 Creative Ways to find Parties

1.) *Pass out catalogs everywhere you go—doctors, dentist, hairdressers, etc.*
2.) *Send out flyers or postcards when new products are introduced— follow-up with a phone call*
3.) *Set up displays at hairdressers, nail salons, etc. Give the owner a free gift*
4.) *Advertise in less expensive ways- church or school bulletins*
5.) *Put flyers or mini catalogs on bulletin boards.*
6.) *Offer a free gift to a person who gives you a lead for a party*
7.) *Have a party in Adult community's recreation room. Provide refreshments.*
8.) *Offer fundraisers to schools and daycare facilities in the area*
9.) *Have a display of a show before or after a meeting such as PTA, business women, etc.*
10.) *Ask your husband to bring a catalog or flyer to work*
11.) *Hold a Christmas or Mother's Day shopping day---A "Men Only" party*
12.) *Talk with the sports moms while your child is at practice*
13.) *Call realtors. Make a new home package with 10% off coupons, free Merchandise for hosting a party coupons….*
14.) *Use your merchandise every chance you get to encourage "Where did you get that?" questions*
15.) *Give your merchandise as donations to organizations with a sticker or business card attached.*

Party Plan enriches your life in many ways. There are parties you never forget and people you have parties with every year. They become part of your party plan family. It all starts with asking. I would have missed so many great experiences and memories if I had not stepped out of my comfort zone and asked people to host parties for me.

No matter where you are or what you are doing, there is a potential party at your fingertips. Learn to listen and ask. If you do not date a party with the person next to you, another consultant has an opening to date a party and reap the benefits. Remember, parties truly are everywhere~!

Here is an example of a drawing form for an event or fair:

Your Party Plan Name
Enter to WIN FREE Merchandise!!!!
Must be filled out completely

Name_____

Email address_____

Home Phone_____

Cell Phone _____

Address_____

City_____ST._____ Zip_____

Tell me about specials & new products_____Yes _____No

I'd like information on hosting a party _____Yes _____No
      for FREE merchandise

I'd like information on becoming _____Yes _____No
an in home consultant

Chapter 5
Unforgettable Parties

The more fun people have at your party, the more likely they are to want to join the fun by hosting one of their own or attending another one. The goal is not only to have a successful party now but to perpetuate your business and create the desire for **your** parties. There are many variations of parties; some add more fun; some increase your sales and income; some are to recognize top hostesses and customers. Whatever kind of party you are doing, make an impression!

Guests at parties come for several reasons–they want to socialize with friends and family; they need to get out of the house; they want to see their friends' new house....... That is the first time they attend. Repeat customers are returning because they like the product but, more importantly, they had FUN at the last party. If you are having fun, the rest falls into place. Similar merchandise can be found just about anywhere—in stores or online. Parties provide an unusual and enticing shopping experience.

For years, I did the traditional party games with average results. Many of the games did not receive great reception. Groans and expressions of dread sometimes permeated the air. The guests certainly did not look forward to them at all. At that time, no other alternative existed. It almost seemed like a necessary evil; once the games ended, the guests relaxed. They loved to receive the unique game prizes but not playing the frivolous games.

Then, at a national convention many years ago, a top manager in sales introduced us to a whole new way to do parties without using those worn out games. I have been doing it at parties ever since. While it is technically still a game, it is a very interactive, exciting one. Guests do not feel self-conscious or apprehensive. They actually enjoy it and look forward to it. It is known as the Auction.

Once I started doing it at some parties, hostesses requested it for their own parties. People held parties that never had before.

My line up of parties was fantastic. I found new consultants at a much faster rate. Gone were the days of cajoling, begging, and pleading for people to host parties. They actually volunteered to host a party. My calendar often filled up faster than I wanted it to. The only activity I use at my parties is the auction party. Everyone has so much fun and looks forward to it. One time I thought my hostesses and guests might need a change of pace so I came with other activities planned. The consensus was, "Why aren't you doing the auction party?" I use it exclusively now.

The Auction

There are many benefits to an Auction party. Everything is easier---doing the demonstration as well as finding parties and consultants. Once you understand and practice the Auction Party format, parties run smoother and the stress of dating parties is almost non-existent. Since the demonstration and the game are one, the time spent in front of the guests is shorter which lengthens their shopping time and your individual interaction with them. The guests get more and more excited as the demonstration progresses and they want more and more money. When you offer $500 or $1000 to host a party at the end, they are hooked! They forget it is play money.

The first time you do the auction, most guests do not know enough about how the game works. The more parties they attend, the more excitement is generated by the ones who know about the auction and are earning extra auction money. Once it becomes your standard party, many people bring outside orders and uninvited guests to the party in order to earn the extra 100s they know is offered. When hostesses' friends bring their friends and/or orders from work etc, and then the hostess calls everyone to invite personally and has outside orders herself, your parties are a tremendous success.

To set up for the auction, the bidders need money. For this you need play money in $100 bill denominations. You can usually find these in toy stores or dollar stores. It is better to have too much money than to run out so I suggest copying the fake bills to ensure you have enough. Always keep a master copy to replenish money when it wears out. You also need enlarged $500 and $1000 bills. Sometimes you can find these in stores but you can also simply enlarge the $100s on a copier and change the 1 to a 5 for $500 and add a 0 for the $1000 bills. These bills should be five or six times larger than the $100 bills. These larger bills are used for dating the parties and they need to look impressive.

Before the party, make sure the hostess knows you are doing the auction party. If she has never been to an auction party, explain how it works and incentivize the hostess to excite the guests prior to the party. She can offer extra money for certain things increase her attendance, sales, and parties.

Having guests bring:
✓	Orders besides your own	$200 each
✓	Bring an uninvited adult guest	$200 each
✓	Bring your invitation	$100

You can incentivize the hostess to work for extra auction money by doing things like:

✓	Calling to invite everyone	$500
✓	Having outside orders	$500
✓	People who want to host a party	$500 each party

You need at least 3-4 guests for the auction to work. When you are ready to start the demonstration, introduce yourself and thank your hostess. Then tell the guests, "We are going to have an auction party." Ask if anyone has attended one before and then explain to those who have not that the object of the game is to accumulate as much money as possible during the course of the demonstration. At the end the demonstration, we have an auction and there are gifts and prizes to bid on.

Present each guest with a $100 bill just for coming to the party. This launches the excitement---you are giving away money! Then award all the guests the extra money they earned for bringing guests, orders, and their invitation with them. Finally, award your hostess her extra money. Make sure you make a big deal when you present the hostess with her money. This is another enticement for others to want to host a party of their own.

In order to jump start the excitement, I give them more $100's before I start demonstrating.

You can make up your own or use the following list award more money.

> *First to arrive*
> *Who traveled the furthest?*
> *Person with the most children*
> *Person with no children*
> *Anyone who has grandchildren*
> *Anyone wearing a specific color*
> *Who cooked dinner before you came?*
> *Who likes to cook?*
> *Anyone who collects_____*
> *Anyone who has already started Christmas shopping*
> *Add any fun question you want!*

Now you are ready to begin the demonstration. I hand the stack of $100's to the hostess and tell her she can play as well. Give them 2 key words to listen for in order to earn more $100s. You can use a seasonal word such as Christmas or a generic word like Gift, but make sure the second word is always **FREE.** The emphasis is to entice the guests to date parties so free merchandise should be on everyone's mind. Decide on 3 identical words to use when they hear these key words—Ho Ho Ho (Christmas) or Fun, Fun, Fun. They shout these out whenever they hear one of the key words to get their $100!

The ones who receive money are the ones who immediately shout it-This may be one, several, or all of them. Usually this gets everyone really warmed up. They may start slow but it does not take long for them all to be yelling out to get $100 bills. As you do your demonstration, make a conscious effort tsay your 2 key words. The object of the game is to create as much enthusiasm as possible and award a lot of $100s. The more you say the words, the louder the guests scream out. Even timid guests join in the pandemonium and have a great time. Unlike other party games, it is a team sport and no one is singled out to do or say anything. At many parties, I would get caught up in the fun and not realize I had said one of the words until the room erupted! At the conclusion of the demonstration, of course, is the auction.

Once you finish the demonstration, tell them they do not have to listen for the key words anymore. Remind them again what the hostess is working toward and that she needs people to host a party to help her achieve her goals. Tell them to count their money without telling anyone how much they have! After you give them a couple minutes to count, go around individually and ask each guest to host a party to help the hostess and they receive $1000 in auction money to spend at the auction. If they hesitate, say "How about $500 to think about it?" Most take it. When you add up her order, you can talk with her alone about having a party.

Now it is time for the auction. Have them count their money and remind them that they cannot share their money. I have 1 ½ times the amount of game gifts to guests (If there are 6 people, I have 9 gifts). These gifts are dollar store items, clearance or anything that is not real expensive. This is where the guests get crazy bidding on items, then laughing about spending $3000 on a bunny figurine. Sometimes the bidding starts slow and you have to joke around with them saying things such as; "Remember this is not REAL money!" Once you get them going, watch out.

It is not unusual to come away from an auction party with 3-4 parties. Potential hostesses in the height of the Christmas season complained about the lack of available dates to have a party. Sometimes we spent time finding a place to put a party. A good problem to have!!

Out of the Box Party Alternatives

The more parties you hold, the more familiar you are with hostesses' preferences. Get in the habit of offering the following alternative parties. Some of them are quick and easy and some of them incorporate places that are fun. There are even many unique suggestions that entice a few highly energetic hostesses to hold a party like no one else. The more options you offer, the better chance there is of finding one to fit each potential hostess.

Office Lunch hour or After Work Party

This is for the person who works and does not have time to hold an in home party or most of the guests live a distance from the hostess' house. Many offices are allowing these kinds of parties. You have the opportunity to see more people. They are already at work so attendance is usually better which typically results in higher sales. The benefit to the hostess is she usually just needs to send out an office email or memo. She does not have to clean her house, her guests are already there, and the parties are normally done quicker with less effort. People usually wish to see the product, make out their order, and get back to work or home depending on the time of day. Refreshments and clean-up are minimal.

Depending on whether the party is held after work or during the lunch hour, the length of the demonstration and amount of products you bring along may need condensing. It is very important to completely plan what the hostess wants or is required to do at an office party. You can work with almost any stipulation or request; the key is to know ahead of time.

Encourage the hostess to circulate the catalog or your website to friends and family outside of the office prior to the party. Most people have friends, family, and neighbors outside of the work environment. The office environment is generally prohibitive to collecting orders after the actual party. If the co-workers did not order or attend, they normally are not going to order anything.

Time constraints can pose a problem if you do not adequately plan. In other words, if you only have an hour for the entire party, make sure your demonstration is shorter to plan time for shopping and completing orders. If you know another reliable consultant, you might consider another hand to help with orders. Remember, it is not only about collecting orders. A successful consultant offers guests the opportunity to host a party of their own. This perpetuates your income and earns the hostess more free merchandise. Just because there is less party time should not mean less new parties in your datebook.

With practice and patience, office parties can become a fun party alternative. After holding two or three, you learn what works and what does not work. If you persist, the results are exciting and rewarding.

Stop and Shop

This is similar to the office party except workers stop at the hostess' house on the way home from work. This is another alternative if the office where she works does not allow parties. Her co-workers are already out and they can make a quick stop before heading home. This is great for co-workers that travel long distances to work and would normally decline an invitation that would require them to make a long drive back to attend. If the hostess lives near work, it is an easy stop for everyone on their way home

With a stop and shop there are no rules and regulations and usually no time constraints. But there is one big challenge. The guests are continually arriving and departing. If you do get a time for a demonstration, it is usually very short and often interrupted several times by arrivals or departures. There may be guests you do not get to speak with directly. It is imperative to get the order forms completely filled out. If you do not talk directly to a guest, you should call to go over the order and talk to them about hosting a party.

A stop and shop seems like an easy way to do a party but it is one of the most challenging and inefficient. I only offered these as a last resort. Since people are on their way home from a long day, they are in a BIG hurry. Some leave the order with the hostess and tell her to let them know the total later. Guests are shortchanged without seeing a full demonstration of the merchandise. The demo gives the opportunity for them to see items they did not notice in the catalog or another use for a product. It is the fun part of the party which is all but eliminated. It truly should only be offered when there is no alternative for a hostess but it always better than losing a hostess.

Pizza Place Party

This type of party is for the hostess who does not want to clean her house or has a very small apartment and many friends. The hostess does not have to fuss. She orders the pizza and soda and the pizza place does the rest—preparation, serving and clean up. These parties usually generate more guests and you can bring a much larger display.

There are many advantages to this party alternative in addition to the housekeeping and refreshment perks. Seldom do you walk away with any less than double your normal party average since the attendance is larger and the excitement as well.

The Auction Party is much more fun. At theses parties, there are usually tables full of guests. More guests= higher sales and more new parties. And happier hostesses!

Couples Party

Inviting the husband may seem like a crazy idea. What man wants to go to an in home party for a bunch of women? Actually, quite a few …. Offer a BBQ, liquid refreshment, and tell them the others are already going and you have a couple's party. Make it enticing, peek their curiosity and provide lots of fun. The big advantage to couples parties is actually the husband. The wife does not have to wonder whether she should buy an item. Many times, men suggest additional items for the wife to buy that she did not notice or considered too expensive. If her husband had not come she may have forgone the item.

Most men are leery of women's get-togethers but if there are other men in the same situation and they are more comfortable. A couple's party generates much laughter and light-hearted joking. It is amazing how much the husbands enjoy the Auction. When a couple's party goes well, repeat parties are almost a guarantee. In fact, many couples look forward to hosting another party!

Accelerators

The preceding party variations supplement your already existing parties. They enable you to do parties at times and places you normally would not be having parties, increasing your sales and adding variety to your schedule. There are other party alternatives that can dramatically increase your sales per party— your hourly wage. They require more work but the payoff is fantastic. These are called accelerators; they put your sales into overdrive. Normally, these parties generate more income and increase your future income (parties). The next parties require more work on your part than the previous party types. They help you to work smarter and usually result in larger sales volumes. Some may double or even triple your average party sales. If you leave the house, you want to earn the highest paycheck possible.

Multiple Hostess Party

These parties have the potential for tremendous results. If the timing is right and you do the required work needed for a successful party, the sales you can generate from this kind of party are truly amazing. These events need to be planned as a theme party or a bingo. The more of them you do, the more people want to be invited. You do not want to do them too often. They need to be special and anticipated. Keep them waiting for the next one! One of the most successful techniques for multiple hostesses is a themed party. It makes the party fun and unique. People love to attend and attendance grows each year as the word spreads about these celebrations. They can be extravaganzas or simple events. These types of parties require commitment and persistence. If you want to double or triple your income, you need to increase the amount of time devoted to this party. If you do not put in extra time, your attendance is low and so are your sales.

Here are some theme ideas:

> Luau
> Mardi Gras
> Patriotic
> Mexican Fiesta
> Italian Festival
> Western BBQ
> St. Patrick's Day
> Christmas or Halloween
> Chinese New Year

You need a good amount of decorations, gifts, and costume accessories. Online websites offer excellent, inexpensive decorations to create your theme. Another good way to acquire decorations are the after holiday sales. Many of the themes you choose are seasonal and stores clear out their supplies each year. Most of the decorations can be reused. Once you have initially planned a theme party, it is easier to execute the next time. Encourage everyone to come dressed in the theme for extra auction money

Decide on a theme and choose a date that is about 4-6 weeks away. You need adequate time to plan the event. Six weeks is the furthest out it should be planned. Otherwise your hostesses lose momentum. There is a fine line between not enough time and too much time. You want them to feel a slight crunch of time to gather orders. If it is planned too far in advance, people procrastinate and even forget. It is better to err on the side of limited time rather than extended time.

Promote the multiple party everywhere you go. You need 25-30 people collecting orders for the party to be a success. Invite people to collect an amount you determined to receive a guaranteed amount of free merchandise. Make sure it is around $100-$125. You have to do the percentage figures for your company to make sure the ratio is correct for sales vs. free merchandise.

Let them know that is the minimum they can receive but the higher the sales, the more free merchandise and drawing tickets they receive. Plan to have several free drawings and a cash giveaway. The cash award should be based on the final amount of sales generated for the entire party. As the sales increase so does the cash! Encourage people to attend even if they don't want to collect orders. Guests receive drawing tickets, may purchase merchandise, are potential hostesses, and add to the excitement.

You must be sure at least 10 people that are collecting orders attend your event. Otherwise there will not be enough sales or people to generate the excitement needed. You are spending more time and money than on an average party. Make sure the amount you earn outweighs the free or discounted merchandise you are offering. The minimum party you are planning is $1000 in combined sales. With most party plans this is the level to receive even greater rewards. Assume the party finishes at $1000 and set free merchandise accordingly.

Most companies have specials, contests, and discounts on merchandise where you can acquire extra merchandise. You need to have several drawings for FREE merchandise for the attending guests and hostesses. The last drawing I always do is cash. People love free merchandise but they ADORE money! I always remind them that I must have at least a certain level of sales for the cash drawing.

Just as you coach your hostesses to call everyone to remind them, you are now the hostess and must do the same thing. It is crucial you maintain contact with the people who agreed to collect orders. Call them 10 days to 2 weeks before the party to see how they are doing on collecting orders and jog their memories about collecting orders if they haven't started. At this point, they still have plenty of time to start passing the catalog around for orders if they have forgotten. Then you MUST call 5 days ahead for a final count. Remember, you need at least 10 hostesses. Finally, call people who just want to attend and not be one of the hostesses.

The day of the party you have to decorate, set up displays and either prepare or pick up the food. It is almost impossible to run these parties alone. Orders need to be tallied, drawing slips filled out for the different promotions, and customers greeted and helped. If you have teenagers or grown children they can assist you and earn some merchandise for their help. An even better solution is to have your consultants help to learn how to run one themselves. Whatever avenue you choose, enlist some help from somewhere. You are going to need it!

Plan the approximate length of time allotted for each part of the party. Flexibility is a necessity since some portions of the program may take more time the larger the attendance. But when you plan the sequence of events, your multiple party runs much smoother. It is quite all right to put time constraints on the amount of time for browsing at the beginning of the party. Usually, I announce, "In 10 minutes I am starting the auction. After the demonstration you are more than welcome to shop more" Start on time! There is always time to shop after the demonstration.

Guidelines for the Party:

***Create the mood
- ❖ Make sure you dress accordingly:
- ❖ Have music playing that will add to the atmosphere
- ❖ Cook or buy theme foods
- ❖ Use balloons and steamers to add to other theme decorations
- ❖ Free giveaways that reflect the theme
- ❖ Hand out an accessory to everyone who attends such as a lei, beads,,

***As guests and hostesses arrive, tally the orders each individual collected, give them a form to fill out for their free merchandise, but leave the final tally until after the demonstration. If you total it now, the guest/hostess may purchase more items and therefore be entitled to more free items. By tallying the orders as they walk through the door, it eliminates mass confusion at the end when everyone wants to leave.

***Have your helper award drawing tickets for all the promotions you are running such as a ticket for:

$125 (whatever the entry level is)
Additional ticket for each $25 in orders over the entry level

Bringing an uninvited guest
Dressing in theme clothing or accessories
Dating a party

***Let guests browse, visit, and enjoy refreshments for the first 30 minutes. Start on time!

***Do the auction and introduce new products, if any, and the specials. Insert pieces of paper into helium filled balloons. If a person decides to host a party, they break the balloon and whatever item is listed I bring to their party as an extra free gift for them.

***After all the excitement from the drawings, encourage shopping and finish the total for each person. Make sure each and every order is filled out completely.

Since it was springtime, I decided to theme my multiple party-Mardi Gras. I found 26 people who wanted to collect orders. I sent out invitations to individual people and promoted it everywhere I went. By the time I began my final calling, I felt cautiously optimistic.

I decorated the house with purple, gold and green Mardi Gras decoration. I made King Cake and pralines. I had New Orleans music playing. My daughter agreed to help me. Thank goodness. I could not believe how many people came. At 1:00 cars pulled up and people dressed in themed attire stepped out. One lady was dressed from head to toe in purple and green with a big purple boa around her neck.

I tallied up each hostess's order as she came through the door. My daughter distributed drawing tickets as fast as she could. The living room and dining room were filled with new spring merchandise. Our guests could browse and eat munchies in the kitchen. All 3 rooms flowed with people.

Finally, everyone was checked in and we were ready for the auction party demonstration. There weren't enough chairs! People had to sit on the floor but they did not seem to mind. They were having so much fun. I had helium balloons floating above their chairs. I finished the auction and it was time for the drawings. These ladies were so jazzed!

We started with the smallest drawing and finished with the cash drawing. The lady who won the cash almost cried; she was so happy. At this point I informed them that the balloons above their heads each had a piece of paper inside with a different item from the new catalog in it. If they would like to put a date in my book for a later party, they could break a balloon and I would bring the extra free gift to their party.

> *Here are the results of this Mardi gras party:*
> - *45 in Attendance*
> - *$3400 in sales*
> - *15 new parties*
> - *2 new consultants*
> - *Priceless amount of free advertising for my next multiple party.*

I would never have guessed my first one would be such a success. It was such a hit that people began to ask me if they could be invited to my next one and the ones who did attend kept telling me not to forget to invite them again. Each time I did another one it was better. Eventually I had to move it to a hall in order to accommodate all the people who wanted to attend.

Bingo

Bingo parties are similar to the multiple parties except each hostess has her own individual party and is rewarded according to her own sales. To qualify, a party must reach the minimum required with your company. Hostesses collect orders and invite their guests to the bingo party. It is held in a hall or at a pizza place Each hostess has her own table for her guests to sit at. Each hostess brings cookies, brownies, finger foods for her table. You provide drinks and paper goods. There are tables for guests who have been invited by you and do not have a hostess (I will tell you how to handle their sales later). Each person who wants to play bingo pays $1-2 per card. This will help defray the cost of the bingo prizes.

First do your demonstration. If you do bingo first, many leave before you have a chance to finish. Believe me; they have come for the bingo! After the demonstration, give them time to shop, fill out their orders, and eat. You can circulate around to assist hostesses and promote more parties.

Make sure you set up a separate table for you to do the final wrap-up of each hostess's order. Again, another person to help at this point is invaluable. After you circulate around for questions and booking parties, go to the table so they can come to you when they are ready. Once they bring the orders to you and you have given the final total, let her know how much free merchandise she is entitled to and then let her sit at the end of your table to fill out her order. That way you can continue with the other hostesses who are in line waiting.

For the guests at the no hostess table(s), tally all the orders individually. Add all the orders together for the party total. Whatever free merchandise would have been awarded to a hostess, you award to someone by drawing a name or you can reward 2 or 3 of them by pulling multiple names. Many times you date another party from one or two of these people.

These bingo parties can generate hundreds, sometimes thousands of dollars in sales for you. They are more work but you have the potential to earn substantially more for one night out and some extra preparation time.

Double Hostess Parties

This is one of the easiest ways to increase your party average. It involves two people that are either related or close friends. They host the party together at one of their homes. Get in the habit of offering this option at your parties. This party actually results in less work because you have 2 parties in one time slot. When you are offering the opportunity for someone to host a party and they hesitate or have the excuse, "My house is too small", or "I work too much." listen to interaction with other people. Sometimes that person is there with a good friend or a sister. You can even ask if there is someone she would consider doing a party with. You can say, "Have you ever thought of doing a double hostess party?"

Listen to her answer. Sometimes the friend or sister jumps on the idea and begins to talk her into it. Let them discuss it for a minute and they eventually ask you how it works. One person hosts the party at their house. The other one brings some refreshments; both invite people. Either the sales are split down the middle or each keeps their own guests' orders separate. No matter which way it is done, the combined sales result in a higher party which equates to extra free product for each hostess, larger paycheck for you with a higher hourly wage.

My first double hostess party happened by accident. As usual, I was talking to a potential candidate for a party. She said, "I am never home and I do not have time to clean my house for a party." Her sister, Lorie, said, "You could have it at my house. I don't mind. I am at home on the weekends if you want to have one on a Saturday."

As we continued to hash over the thought, we came up with the idea for them to host it at Lorie's house, Gail would bring desert. Both of them loved the idea so we decided to try it.

I rarely work on Saturdays but I figured this might need to be one of my few exceptions. I did let them know that I did not normally work on weekends. I wanted them to be sure they committed to doing it before I had them decide on a date. So Lorie and Gail began to plan their party. Everyone there assured them they would come to their party.

When I called to make sure their invitations had gone out, Lorie told me they decided to have a brunch so not to eat before I came. The day of the party I walked in to the wonderful aroma of fresh baked cookies, candies and an assortment of delicious food.

It hardly seemed like work. There were 15 people there and the sales finished at double my usual party average. Does it get any better than that?

Appreciation Theme Parties

Honor your Hostesses and repeat customers at a VIP appreciation theme party. They are intended to reward exceptional hostesses and customers. Introduce a new catalog. It creates anticipation since you should only do them once or twice a year. These parties are invitation only events. They need to be special and exciting. You want people to work to be invited and feel special when they attend. The anticipation of a theme party is half the fun.

You are the hostess as well as the consultant for these parties. You must make the atmosphere special to thank your wonderful hostesses and VIP customers for helping with your success. You must do all the things you encourage your hostess to do for her parties. You need to send or hand out invitations and then follow up with a personal reminder call to determine attendance.

The primary purpose for these parties is to reward top hostesses, generate new parties, and introduce new merchandise.

Since there is a significant amount of time and money expended, some profit should be planned into the event. You can offer the opportunity to place an order; purchase discounted discontinued merchandise or both to your hostesses and special guests. It should be a privilege to attend these events. These special guests have the opportunity to take advantage of discounted merchandise. Make sure they understand this distinctive perk. Only top performers are invited to this extravaganza.

Since this is a gathering of top people, you usually book future parties. Your future parties insure income in the coming months. If you date lots of parties, it is a victory!

No matter which game or type of party you choose, make your parties unforgettable. If the hostess and the guests have fun, they want to recreate the atmosphere again and have another party with you.

Party Like You Love It!

MARCH MARDI GRAS
Saturday, March 27th @ 3:00
"The easy way to have a party!"

You don't have to:
> ****Clean your house
> ****Make refreshments
> ****Send out invitations & reminders

How does it work?
> ****Collect at least $100 in orders (before tax/shipping)
> ****Bring the orders and any friends that would like to attend with you
>> That's it!!!

What do you receive?
> **** A guaranteed $25 in merchandise for each $100 in orders you have
> ****Mardi Gras Munchies made by ME
> ****See a display that has EVERY item I have (over $1500 at this point)
> ****Chances for additional drawings ($500 in free & specials!)

> ### SEVEN DRAWINGS!!!!
>> $50.00 CASH
>> $75 Garden Mist Fountain
>> $50 Stainless Steel Utensil Set
>> Singing Sonny & Cher Frogs
>> Option to purchase the March Specials

Of course we will have the auction party for more fun prizes
Here's how you can get extra Mardi Gras money:

Every $100 in orders	$500
Bring an adult guest	$200each
Mardi Gras Attire	$200
beads, mask, etc.	
Book a home show	$1000
Listen to the job opportunity	$500

Please RSVP as we need at least 10 people to participate!!!!

Chapter 6
Control your Business

Learning to control your business is just as challenging and equally as important as the parties themselves. You are your own boss. Since you are the boss as well as the employee, you must make the employee step up and do what is necessary to succeed. You must manage your datebook, your stress, and continually make new goals. A smoothly running business needs a balanced schedule that does not cause stress and is moving in a positive direction.

The first step to taking control is to manage your datebook so it does not control your life. Your date book is your business and personal planner. While it seems like simple concept, it can quickly get out of control if you do not monitor it. You need to plan as well as record, both your personal and business activities. Do not rely on your memory for even the most basic commitments. This story is hard to imagine but it actually happened to me.

When I first started to work in party plan, I was grateful for any and all parties so I let them schedule parties wherever they wanted. Before long, I was completely at the mercy of my hostesses. I was working anywhere from 6 to 7 days a week. We never had an entire weekend to do anything.

At this point I decided I needed to prioritize my life. My family must always come first. I made weekends off limits. I wrote in obligations every Saturday and Sunday. When the prospective hostess looked in my datebook for a day for her party, weekends were taken. I soon discovered that most people do not have to hold their party on a weekend. All my hostesses soon understood weekends were my family time and respected it. At times, I have been very busy and had to put in many hours into the business. I worked extra hours all week but my weekends normally remained free to relax with my family.

I think that is why I stayed in party plan so long. I learned to schedule my personal time with as much priority as my business time. My hostesses remembered, "No weekends, right?" My family knows they always come first and my hostesses value me enough to happily comply. Everyone is happy, especially me.

But one time I did not follow my own system. Although I usually documented all my personal commitments in my date book, one March I got behind and went to my first party without entering everything. In the excitement of the party, I made a huge mistake. Upon returning home, I realized I had booked a party on my own birthday.

At first, I thought I should just do it and celebrate my birthday another day. My husband gently reminded me of my family first rule. Luckily, it was a friend of mine and she gladly changed the date of her party. We had a good laugh. She understood but it was a very unprofessional thing to do.

In addition to recording all personal and business dates, I strongly suggest you color code them with a highlighter so you can tell at glance what the date represents. You can do what works for you. I use yellow for anything business related, blue for personal & kids, and green for appointments such as the doctor or dentist. There is no one telling you what you must accomplish each day. That is entirely up to you. Your datebook is the place to enter everything you need to accomplish in a day/week/month. You decide how much you want or need to work. It is very easy to let work overtake play time---everyone needs time to decompress. If you need to schedule it to make it happen, write it in a time slot just as you would any other obligation.

The color code system helps you determine where you need improvement. You can tell at a glance if you need to change your scheduling. If your goal is to work 3 or 4 times a week, there should be at least 3 yellow highlighted commitments. If there is no blue in the schedule, add some personal down time. Balance is the key to a happy consultant—and family.

It is also a very good idea to have a second calendar in your phone. If you leave the physical datebook at a party, you do not want to frantically try to figure out your schedule or drive all the way back to a hostess' house especially if she is a distance away.

The physical datebook is so I can have the hostess sign her own date in my book. It helps eliminate errors in name and phone number. It creates accountability. The phone calendar is at your fingertips for backup or quick checking what you have scheduled BUT you must update it.

Working from home allows flexibility and many benefits. However, when working from home, it is easy to spend empty, unproductive time at the computer, on the phone or doing busy work. There are pitfalls to working at home that can steal time and prevent success. It takes time and practice to take control of your business. If you find yourself getting off track, take a deep breath and get realigned. Not one consultant I know is perfect in every area. The trick is to recognize where you need improvement and work on it.

Managing Stress

Stress is part of the job description when you are self-employed. The key is to recognize bad stress and how to overcome or manage it. No matter what your business, usually you are required to juggle many tasks at once. We call this multi-tasking. Too much multi-tasking can lead to high levels of stress. When you are out of control of a situation, you constantly feel tired and overwhelmed. Ultimately, you feel guilty that you are not productive. These feelings create stress---bad stress. Bad stress needs to be managed. If it continues over long periods of time, it can lead to burnout. Burnout is counterproductive in any job but is especially damaging to self employed people. Here are indications you are on a stressful, destructive path:

> ➤ Not doing the calls, contacts, or tasks needed
> ➤ Excessive procrastination
> ➤ Irritability with family and friends---you hear "What's wrong?' frequently
> ➤ Excessive negativity

- ➤ Feeling overwhelmed with simple tasks so you start nothing
- ➤ Easy to provoke
- ➤ Feel tired much of the time
- ➤ Feel like your world is ready to crumble
- ➤ Self-esteem is suffering
- ➤ Depression
- ➤ Guilt that you should accomplish more or should be doing a task you are not doing.
- ➤ Not enough time to finish daily tasks—always running behind whether it is paying bills or meeting deadlines

The more of these symptoms you have, the more likely you are either burnt out or headed in that direction. After you recognize the problem, you can begin to solve it.

There are ways to dramatically reduce stress and improve your attitude, prosperity, and health.

- ➤ Eat healthier
- ➤ Avoid excesses such as drinking, overeating, smoking, etc
- ➤ Exercise regularly(The more exercise you get the more energy you have)
- ➤ Delegate at home and work
- ➤ Determine what is important and do not worry over insignificant tasks---eliminate the guilt
- ➤ Prioritize all aspects of your life
- ➤ Read motivational books
- ➤ Find time for yourself every day
- ➤ Evaluate your current situation and eliminate the stress producers
- ➤ If possible, take a short break or mini vacation

Organizing your office and your record keeping are necessities for an efficiently run business. As a consultant you work from multiple offices—your home office, your car, and the hostess' home.

Home office

Setting up your office and maintaining organization once it is set up, is vitally important to your business. A little bit of time preparing your business tools ahead of time is worth twice as much time later. If you keep a constant stock of necessary tools, you are not caught short.

Even though most people create files on their computer, you need some type of backup system. A file cabinet for all original paperwork such as hostess party order, guest order forms, and any kind of certificates works well. Each hostess should have an open folder until you complete the party. Then you can file it in a common file listed by party number or alphabetically.

- Parties—current info on hostesses for the week, phone# and sales.
- Phone log & Leads—Enter the person you talked to, where, date and time, and any notes to help refresh your memory when you talk to her again
- Promotions & Contests—Weekly or monthly flyers with specials, bonuses, hostess incentives and any other promotions.
- Correspondence—a running list of hostesses and a column to check when you complete a thank you to your hostess after the party.
- Fairs and Shows—List of upcoming events at which you are displaying merchandise and another list of events, date and contact numbers of those you are considering..

A very important part of your home office is your tax records. Since you are in business as an independent contractor, you must keep an accurate account of your expenses and deductions. If you get into the habit of recording everything as it happen, it does not become an insurmountable chore at the end of each year. With the extensive list of items that need tracking, you become overwhelmed without a system of recordkeeping. There are many apps for your phone to help you track things like mileage and expenses.

If you are not sure whether something is a deduction for your business or not, keep the receipt or scan it into your computer tax filing system. Then talk to your accountant or tax advisor.

Invest in an expense account record keeping book or program every year and enter your expenses either immediately or at the end of each week. I use a combination of computer and manual bookkeeping.

If I incur an expense at home, I immediately record it and file or scan the receipt. If not, I have a manila envelope with a notebook that I keep with my car. I place the receipt in the envelope after scanning it into my phone. At the end of the week, remove all the receipts, and enter them in the master record keeping book/tax record keeping program. This simple habit translates to less stress, usually more money, and great time savings. If you are in business for yourself, good record keeping results in extra monetary benefits at tax time.

Portable Office/ Car Office

More than likely, you spend a large amount time on the road away from your home office. You store a large amount of items in your car. If you are not careful, your car can become a cesspool of chaos. You throw things on the seat, have little to no organization, and have a hard time finding anything. It is easy to find yourself in this situation. A few small changes in procedure can almost eliminate the disaster that is your car office.

Here are some organization ideas:
*Use crates and plastic tubs for extra hostess packets, folders, and any extra paperwork.
 *Tubs carry extra auction gifts and samples.
 *Most of the merchandise can be kept in suitcases for parties. If you change the merchandise, bring the suitcases in, change the merchandise, sometimes set it up, and then return the newly packed suitcases to the car. It is always packed and ready to go.
 * In a more accessible area, preferably in the front, keep a stock of business cards and flyers, a few catalogs, and any other pertinent paperwork.

Ideally, your car should have most of the extra supplies you might need at a party. When you have your car organized; you can quickly run out and get more catalogs, auction gifts, hostess packets, etc. Also, if you are training a new consultant, you can send them out to get the supplies and not worry that they won't be able to locate what you need.

Goals

Always set goals. Make them measurable and attainable. Without a goal, you never have a sense of accomplishment. Each time you set a goal, it should excite and invigorate you, not frustrate you to the point of feeling defeated. Sometimes a goal needs readjusting. Better to have lowered the goal and reached it, than to leave the bar so high you give up and do not try again. Even when you fall short of your goal, you stretched further than you would have without it and each time you set another goal you come closer to meeting and sometimes surpassing the goal.

Goals should be stepping stones. As you reach one stone (goal), you stretch to the next and the next and the next. Before you know it, you have reached a level you believed impossible. The object of setting a goal is to make you stretch, not break. Dream big but break it down into small attainable pieces. Once you know what it is you really want, take the first step and keep going.

A good salesperson always welcomes competition. Top performers covet the #1 spot. Healthy, positive competition is good for you. It forces you to be the best you can be. You must do what you do even better than before to succeed. Each time you are the winner in a competition, your confidence soars. Every time you lose, your determination rises. When you stretch to do more than your competitor, you improve your own performance. The more you stretch, the higher sales you generate, the higher your income. Eventually, you reach, and many times, surpass the goal.

You cannot rest on your successes anymore than you can give in to your defeats. Top salespeople experience both. They learn from both as well. When you make a mistake or a situation causes you to fail, you learn from the experience and move forward.

Goals are a very important part of any sales organization. The one I worked for believed you should stretch your limits. One manager meeting mainly centered on our goals. We wrote down our group monthly goals and shared them. Almost every manager wrote down they wanted to attain the top sales level. This is the answer the distributor expected.

I have to admit, I do like to go against the grain but that is not why I chose one sales level below that as my goal. I believed I had chosen an attainable goal. Top level would require months of preparation, goal setting and encouragement. To expect an $8,000 increase in one month seemed ludicrous.

The goal I set for my group required a $4000 increase over the previous month. It still might be too much, but I felt we at least had a chance of succeeding with this goal. To attain that level, the group would really need to stretch their limits.

Many managers come to me after the meeting and remarked in amazement, "You don't want to be a Top Manager?!" I explained that I wanted the goal attainable and that I felt my group would get discouraged at an unrealistic goal. I knew the group could get there eventually but not in one month. They listened to me but I could tell they thought I sold myself and my group too short. I stood firm---and alone. I am sure no one agreed with my reasoning.

At my group meeting, I recounted what happened at the manager meeting. In essence, I put them on the spot. They needed to show everyone we could do it. Not one of them wanted our group to look incompetent so they all committed to do the best job possible. Each consultant created a goal and I shared mine. If we reached our individual goals, we could reach our goal.

Every consultant worked extremely hard that month. At the end of the month, the consultants called in their monthly report. As each call came in, my excitement grew. Closer and closer we inched toward the goal. That month my group sold over $14,000 in merchandise. Only 2 managers attained their goal— one at the Top level and the other—my group. Of course, our next goal did become Top Level!

How do you set and meet a goal? Decide what it is that you are working toward. Write it down and begin to create a plan to meet it. What is your party average? How much sales do you need to do? Are there other avenues in addition to sales that are available to you such as recruiting or bonuses? At this point, assess the feasibility of the goal. If it is out of the realm of possibility, adjust your goals and redo your plan. Do not discard this dream, set it on the back burner for later consideration. Not now does not mean never.
The steps for setting and attaining goals are:
1.) Set your sights high
2.) Dream big but break it down into smaller, attainable goals
3.) Know exactly what you want and go for it.
4.) Commit to achieving it
5.) Tell everyone what your goal is
6.) Keep your goal posted where you can see it
    --If you have a picture of it hang it where you can see it daily
7.) Periodically reevaluate, readjust and redefine your goals
    --What can I do better?
    --Have my priorities changed?
    --Do I still desire the same goal?

**If you reach your goal, celebrate. Splurge on something for yourself or your family. It doesn't matter if it is large or small; just reward yourself for a job well done.
**If you fall short of the goal, reassess it. If you feel you did not put enough effort into reaching it, give yourself another chance; then reset the goal if you do not attain it.

Setting goals is the easy part, working the plan every day to reach it, is difficult. It is extremely easy to make excuses for yourself. No matter what you are doing, procrastination, excuses, and a negative attitude are waiting to ruin your potential successes. A support system is invaluable. Find a fellow consultant to help you keep focused. You can root for each other and hold each other accountable. Write out goals and find pictures of things you want to do and put them up all over the house to keep you motivated. Whatever works to keep you on pace for your goal—do it!

No matter what the goal is, you need to continue to do it and do your best. Everyone's best is different. You know when you are doing your best and when you are not. Most people have good intentions. Successful people not only have good intentions, they also have great implementation. They work toward their goal every day. They reassess their goals when necessary and examine what they could improve in order to reach the goal they set for themselves.

If you fall short of your goal, there are always negative people to let you know you have fallen short. Negative people want company in their misery. When a person says it cannot be done, it means they believe they cannot do it. Some of the most successful people fell short of their goals again and again. It is not that you fall down; it is how many times you get back up and try again. People who are unwilling to let go of their dreams, succeed.

Goals give you a feeling of accomplishment and reinforce positive attitude. When you occasionally fall short of the goal, it should make you more determined. The most important thing to remember about goals is to set them higher than you are now but not so high that you are defeated before you start. Once you set a goal, you must commit to doing your best otherwise, it is not a goal; it is a dream. There is no better feeling in the world than the sense of accomplishment and pride you feel once you complete a tough goal.

Chapter 7
Time Management

Time management is a way of life. Everyone knows a person who can accomplish double what the average person does in a day. Yet, they rarely appear stressed. They have learned the beauty of controlling time instead of letting time control them. Since you are your own boss, possessing time management skills is vital. If you do not currently utilize time efficiently, work on acquiring skills to help make better use of your time. You cannot get more time in your life; you need to manage it wisely. If you are in high stress mode, there is usually little or no time management. In order to decrease stress levels, more time management is a necessity.

Time management is working and playing smarter---not harder. It is prioritizing your life and what is important or necessary. When time is spent doing low priority tasks or busy work, valuable time is lost that can never be regained. Prioritizing is critical for all aspects of your life. The less time business takes, the more time can be spent on fun and recreation.

Time management is especially necessary for an efficiently run, profitable business. Good time management produces maximum income potential. Once you have time management skills, you can accomplish much more than most with less effort. Time Management is self-discipline and organization. It is the choice of achieving what you really want by doing things you don't really want to do. It is setting priorities; learning to delegate and constantly reevaluating your priorities. The ultimate goal is to become a more efficient you.

Cramming it all into one day does not work. We have become a society who needs everything done yesterday. We rush to work, rush to the store, rush home, rush the kids to activities, rush relationships, and sleep less in our rush to start the next day. The feeling of urgency pervades every aspect of our life. We believe the faster we go, the more we can cram into one day. No matter how much time we have, we need to go faster; do more.

Unfortunately, if you live like this on a regular basis, your effectiveness eventually wanes; your health may suffer, and you never have enough time in one day to complete all of your tasks.

There is a difference between what you feel is important and doing what you think should be important. Sometimes we ignore our inner signals and choose to do something else. Not only can this result in spinning your wheels but it is time wasted. Once you have decided a task is a priority, you feel guilty when you are not devoting enough time to accomplishing it. This starts the guilty conscience syndrome. It happens when you push tasks aside to do what you thought you should or do not take time to do things that are important or necessary

Make sure when you accept a commitment or task that you truly have the time and desire to accomplish it. You must complete it, which is taking time from your schedule, pass the job to someone else or make an excuse to the person who gave it to you in the first place. When asked to do something, take a step back and honestly evaluate whether you have the time or desire to do it. When you do not honor a commitment, you feel a sense of failure and may resort to excuses. It is far better to refuse it initially than to worry about it and have it hanging over your head, dragging you down until the due date. You want to be known as a person who can be counted on to complete obligations, not a person that backs out at the last minute.

The first NO is always the hardest. When you stop and really assess whether or not to accept a commitment, you find yourself agreeing only to what you are absolutely sure you can complete. You are happier and have a great feeling of empowerment. You are running your schedule; it is not running you.

Determine your most efficient time of day and utilize it. If the best time of day for you is morning, try to do the most important, high energy, or mentally challenging tasks then. The task takes less time and is done better when you are at your peak performance. Each task that takes less time and energy is more time you have to devote to another project. Sometimes your peak performance does not coincide with your peak workload. That is all right as long as you strive to optimize your most efficient time whenever possible.

Priorities are constantly changing. You need to take stock periodically. Too many priorities keep you frozen. Everything cannot be a priority. If your to do list is too long, you need to re-prioritize. Eliminate, delegate, or reschedule lower priorities. Identify what needs to be accomplished and what is necessary to complete them.

How do you know how to prioritize our daily, weekly, and long term tasks? First, ask yourself 3 questions---"How important is it?"; "Do I need to do it now?"; and, "Is it really necessary?" There are always 1 or 2 tasks that immediately pop into your head when you think about what need to get done in a day. Most generally, these are your important, urgent and necessary tasks. Each person must determine their own high and low priorities and the order in which they are to be started and/or completed. Classify your tasks into 3 categories:

A---<u>Absolutely necessary</u>

A-tasks are the high priority tasks. Some of these tasks have a definite time they need to be done such as meetings, parties, picking up the kids from school, etc.; others are tasks that you decide are a priority such as phone calls. They need to be done now and cannot or should not be postponed. Each task needs to be assigned an approximate timeline. Be sure to limit the amount of these tasks.

There is a fine line between A and B tasks. If a task is in the B category and all A category tasks have been completed, it becomes an A priority. It is better to complete all your A priorities and start on the B list than to fail to complete the A list. When you fail to complete your A list, it causes stress in your life. Usually, you have to relegate them to the next day. The A-task list should be the shortest list in your daily plan. The goal is to complete your A list daily.

B---Borderline

These are secondary tasks. They can or must wait. Some get relegated to "B" status because there are too many tasks on the "A" list. If there is time left after all A list tasks are completed, then tasks in the B list move to the highest priority spot. This is where time management really starts to shine. Just as in anything in the middle, this is the "wiggle room." These tasks could easily be on the A list but either you have enough already or they are not a high priority at this time. It is up to you to decide when these tasks should be done.

Monitor these daily. If you leave some of these tasks for too long of a period they become emergency A tasks.

C---Customize

These tasks are not a high priority and normally never become an A priority. Nevertheless, they need to be completed. You can delegate them. You can also reevaluate when they need to be completed and fit in small time slots. They are tasks that can fit in between other tasks or you have a longer time frame to finish them. These are tasks such as speeches, calls, or intermittent jobs. Many times the tasks on this list are never ending such as laundry. If you have good time management skills, these tasks should rarely progress to the B list. C tasks are the lowest priority and should take the least amount of time and energy. Occasionally, a C task may become a priority, but it should rarely happen.

Normally, a C task becomes a priority only because it has been put off for so long.

Laundry is a perfect example. This is a job that is never ending. It is definitely something that has to get done but can easily be fit in and around most other activities. In between phone calls, dinner preparation, or kid's homework, a load can be put in the washer and then transferred to the dryer. A little more time is needed to fold and put it away but it still is not more than 15-20 minutes at a time.

When you procrastinate, it continues to pile up. Soon it is overflowing the hampers in the house and everyone is complaining about their lack of clothing. At this point it has become an absolute necessity. Everything stops and you spend a few hours catching up.

Now you must spend precious time on a C priority that you could be spending on another A one. Too much procrastination and all tasks can become a priority and this hampers your productivity.

Here are a few habits to develop to keep your personal C tasks in check:

- o Stock up on items that you use frequently
- o Throw laundry in while fixing dinner, doing work
- o Bring bills, and thank you cards to fill out at doctors, dentists. Catch up on business texts
- o Always make double dinners---lasagna, casseroles for later quick fixes
- o Stop to do shopping on the way to or from work instead of using large blocks of time to do it
- o Make out birthday, anniversary cards at beginning of each month
- o Never let your gas tank go below ¼ tank. Fill it up on the way home
- o Anything you can do immediately—do it! Make the bed, do the dishes, etc.

Some habits for business "C" tasks are:

- o Stamping catalogs and business materials
- o Address envelopes and thank you notes
- o Put together packets for hostesses

- o Log expenses and mileage for tax purposes as they occur
- o File receipts and expenses daily or weekly
- o Organize open and closed parties and file them
- o Tend to problems immediately

Here is an example of how setting A-B-C priority works:
    Either before bed at night or first thing in the morning, list your tasks for the day and assign each one an A-B-C priority level and a time allotment (how long you estimate it takes to complete the task). As you start to compile your list, start with the tasks that need a specific time slot. Then progress to all the other A tasks, then B.... filling in your schedule but leaving some room for unexpected interruptions or tasks that take longer to complete than scheduled. The more you work this system, the more efficient you become.

Here is an example of how setting A-B-C priority works:

Monday Tasks:

A Tasks		B Tasks		C Tasks	
Call Hostess	45 min	Finish Orders	45 min	Laundry	30 min
Dentist	2:45 pm	Clean House	1-2 hrs	Get milk	30 min
Pick up kids	4:00pm	Do dishes	30 min	Emails	30-45 min
Party	6:30 pm	Make dinner	30 min	Thank you notes	30 min
Make cookies	1 hr			Texts	15 min
				Plan mtg	30 min

    On this day, almost the entire afternoon is specific time tasks so the morning is the only flexible time period. So from 2:45pm on there is very little room for unplanned tasks. But I do have some possibilities; if the dental visit only takes the average 45 minutes, I have time to run to the store before picking up the kids; if it takes longer, I can do it on the way home from picking them up. I purposely scheduled the dental appointment so I would not encounter a time crunch if the appointment ran longer than usual or the office ran behind schedule. Always allow more than enough time between appointments to all but eliminate the stress that is created when you are late and do not have adequate time to get to your destination.

Monday is the day I chose to maintain many of my weekly household chores but it can easily be changed to another day if a higher priority presents itself. Remember the B task level is where most of the flexibility in your schedule is. The C tasks for this day are ones I can fit in around other things and have not been left so long that they need immediate attention. All of the C tasks have plenty of time left before it develops into a **now** situation.

Once you categorize your priorities for the day, create a timeline for each job. Make sure you allow adequate time for each task.

Here is the tentative timeline for Monday:

8:00-10:00	Clean house—*do laundry*
10:30-11:15	Finish and submit orders for 2 parties
11:15-12:00	Stamp catalogs, do emails/texts
12:00-1:00	Lunch with Sue—*meeting*
1:00-2:00	Make cookies and do dishes
2:00-2:20	Calls
2:20	Leave for dentist
2:45-3:20	Dentist---*thank yous, etc*
3:20-4:00	Go to the grocery store...
4:00-4:30	Pick up kids and drive home
4:30-5:30	Kid time-homework.....*make dinner*
5:30-6:30	Dinner
6:30	Party

This may seem very scheduled but there is actually a lot of room for changes. The tasks in *italics* are done while you are working on another higher priority task. If they are not finished, you can complete them at a later date. With good time management you can complete 2 tasks in the same time frame.

Flexibility and creativity take time management to amazing heights.

Each day is another start. Do not get discouraged if you cannot complete tasks on a given day but do not fall into the trap of putting off overwhelming projects. Almost all large tasks can be broken down into small manageable pieces. Decide which pieces you can delegate, which you need to do yourself. Some tasks are so large that you have to convince yourself to start. Start with the worst part of the task. Once that is complete, the next piece will go easier and the next even easier.

You have decided what your priorities are, scheduled personal time, and made a list. You may have good intentions but if you don't act on them they can never materialize. List making is great but if all you do is make lists you are just wasting time. After you create a list you MUST implement it. Mistakes are okay. It is better to make a mistake when attempting to do something than to do nothing at all.

Organization is vital for an efficiently run, stress free business but action produces results. Even if you are not totally organized, start! You always accomplish more than the person who does not start until the action plan is perfect. Something is better than nothing and practice makes perfect. Also, once you work your plan, you may find better ways to utilize your time and energy. Standing on the outside and judging how a plan works is very ineffective.

The last requirement of time management is to plan for change. Nothing is set in stone. If you expect everything to go as planned, you are setting yourself up to fail and increase your stress level tremendously. Just as the old adage proclaims:

"If it can go wrong it will."

Most of us want our schedule to go as planned. Even when we have flexibility in our day, change causes frustration. We expect to control our day either consciously or unconsciously. There are always bumps in your road but how big that bump is depends on how you handle it. If you see it as a roadblock to what you wanted to accomplish, it is a major stumbling block. If you see it as an adventure or a new challenge it is little more than a hiccup in your day. For easier adjustments to changes in your schedule, allow at least an extra 15 minutes for any errand (lines in the bank, store, etc) Plan at least an extra half hour into the daily schedule for last minute changes.

The outcome of better Time Management should not be more work in a day, but the ability to have more time for play. Good time management gives you a sense of well-being, accomplishment, and satisfaction. It eliminates the guilty conscience and thoughts, "I should be doing...." Time management is a finish line. Each day should start a new goal not be a continuation of the day, week, or month before.

You need to reward yourself for jobs well done. Do not forget what is really important when you are prioritizing your life. Priorities are not only for business. What you value comes first; everything else follows that. Nobody on his deathbed ever says I wish I had spent more time on my business.

1.Promise yourself a reward for completing an especially challenging task. If I get these done, I am going to take the kids out for ice cream or buy myself a new pair of jeans.

2.Schedule personal time. Plan time for this in your schedule on a regular basis. Birthdays, anniversaries, family gatherings, and important events should be scheduled first, then business obligations. If weekends are family time, make sure all your business is conducted during the week.

3.Learn the word "NO." Realizing your limitations is a must for time management. Volunteering or becoming the helpful neighbor can get out of hand No one is going to look out for your interests except you.

4.Limit phone and text time. This is the biggest sabotage of managing your time. When you are working, set a limit for the amount of time you are going to call. The more interruptions you have, the more time you have to spend on your business. A loss of too much personal time ultimately causes problems when you and/or your family start to resent how much time you devote to business.

Time management is an ongoing learning process. You cannot read one book or go to one class and expect to be an expert. It is a habit you build day by day. Sometimes it is hard to manage your time but if you make it a habit, over time it will become less of a chore and more second nature to you. Time management creates a happier, less stressed feeling. You will find you have more time for business and more time for yourself. As your time management skills improve, your goals become more and more attainable. The ability to manage your life is one of the most satisfying, rewarding skills you can acquire.

Chapter 8
Customer Satisfaction = Success

What is a customer? A customer is person who wants and can afford what you offer and has become a customer due to your sales ability and personal charisma. A good salesperson can sell most people anything once. A great salesperson provides such a wonderful experience that they have a large base of repeat customers.

People do not want mass produced, cheaper products. They want quality products as well as, customer service with their purchase. They are willing to search for it. As a salesperson, you need to make sure you do not forget what your business really is--- customers. Without customers, there is no business. Customer loyalty exists when you possess the ability to sell yourself. Be a person with integrity and keep customers happy so they return again and again.

Part of human nature is the need for appreciation. Customers need to feel they are important to you. It does not take much to make them feel appreciated. When you attempt to listen and do not, customers know they are not important to you. They will find somewhere to do business that does make them feel appreciated.

4 Steps for Outstanding Customer Service
1. Determine Customer Type
2. Create a Bond
3. Solve Problems
4. Maintain Contact

The first step to customer satisfaction is to know your customer. Determine what type of customer you are working with. Many salespeople mistakenly assume their customers need and want the same things they do. While this may sometimes be true, often it is far from the truth. There are many types of consumers in the marketplace and every one of them has a different reason for purchasing product.

Bargain Hunter:
Looking for discounted value-priced merchandise. This customer wants the most bounce for their buck. They are willing to wait for a sale and do not need the newest products on the market.

Forerunner:
Wants product the minute it is introduced. This customer is not worried as much about cost as he/she is about being the first one in their circle of friends to own this product.

Utilitarian:
Needs the product to serve a purpose or multiple purposes. This customer is not a frivolous purchaser and very rarely buys on impulse. Sometimes it takes a bit of time for them to decide to buy even the most inexpensive item.

Gadgeter:
Likes products that do something and are fun. That's it!

Value Shopper:
Slightly different from the bargain hunter. The value shopper wants the product to be worth the money. They are not afraid to spend a bit but the product must be worth the cost.

Impulse Buyer:
Purchases product because everyone else is or they like the presentation of it. They may spend too much and may never use the item.

Think about yourself. Suppose you are a Utilitarian; you want products to have a specific use or multiple uses. You do not worry about finding bargains and NEVER impulse buy. On the other hand, your customer is an impulse buyer, frequently grabbing items from end caps while in line to purchase. You start expounding on the multiple uses of a product instead of its allure and flashiness. Your customer loses interest almost immediately and you lose a potential sale. Most products can be presented to fit most buying styles. You need to know which attribute to highlight.

Of course, when you are demonstrating your product at a party, you must address all of the different buyers. Once you are talking to the guests individually, is when your must really listen to determine which type of buyer they resemble. If you let them answer your questions, it usually becomes very apparent what they deem important.

Dress for success is a requirement. First impressions are rarely reversible; project a professional image. When you dress for success you tell your customer that he or she is valued and that you care enough about them to take time to dress well. Professionals do not conduct important business in sweats and sneakers. The clothes you choose every day determine the level of success you are trying to attain. You also feel better and work more productively when you are professionally dressed. Once you develop the habit of dressing for success, you rarely leave the house in unacceptable condition.

In addition to presenting yourself professionally, your manner and integrity must prove you are a person of your word. Back up whatever you promise. Never make an empty promise. Anything for a sale is a dangerous way to do business. Eventually, you are going to have to prove yourself. One irate customer destroys months or possibly, years of customer relations.

Once the customer bond is established, do everything in your power to make them crave your individual style. Make sure they seek you, not settle for any consultant. I created this with the auction party, unusual incentives, and extravagant recognitions. What makes it worth their while to initiate contact with you for a party? Any consultant should not be able to fill your unique niche. Determine why the customer would want to do business with you. What makes your business stand out?

Offer perks! This could be free delivery, extended warranty, a gift for multiple purchases, etc. Anything that makes the customer feels he/she is receiving special treatment. Just make sure it is not excessive. Do not give so much away that you cannot continue to reward similar quantities as your customer base increases. There is so much competition in the marketplace that you need to find a niche. Never forget that a customer is not required to do business with you, they choose to do business with you.

Your job is not complete and the party is not officially closed until the hostess has received her merchandise and everyone is satisfied. In party plan, your hostess is your primary link to most of your guests/customers in addition to being a customer herself. She usually hears the problems and reports them to you. It may be a broken or defective item. It may be that she is simply not happy with the product. Whatever the problem is, she is the messenger and ultimately is responsible for her guests' happiness. These guests are her friends and family and if their problem is not resolved, the hostess feels guilty because she invited them to their home and now they are not happy. If you do not fix the problem, the guest is angry, the hostess is even angrier and you have lost business, credibility and reliability.

A strong, lasting relationship is based on communication. Customers need to feel comfortable communicating problems and complaints to you or their hostess. It is easy to give customer service when everything is going smoothly. Resolving customer problems, shows what kind of company you work for and what kind of businessperson you really are.

Always try to remain positive even when the customer is filled with negativity. If your hostess calls with damaged or missing items, make sure you tend to this **immediately.** Remember, it is the little things that irritate them. You can be the best demonstrator and guests can love the merchandise, but if you do not solve their problems, you fail.

A party plan consultant is a master negotiator. You have to figure out how to resolve any issues that arises. A good listener looks at the person the ENTIRE time they are speaking with the express purpose of understanding what they are trying to convey

Listening is skill rarely developed in today's society. Listening takes time and your total attention. It is not thinking about what to say next, how to solve the problem, a similar experience you have had, etc. It is simply making eye contact with the person, concentrating on what they are saying and then responding.

The purpose of listening is to ask the person questions once they finish not tell them something.

First assess the situation:
>   **Is it a small problem or one that has escalated into a major dissatisfaction?
>   **What does the customer want (replacement, refund, or someone to listen)?
>   **What is the root of the problem?
>   **Can you solve it?

Don't try to explain the reason for the problem or where the fault lies. The customer does not really care why it happened. They just want it corrected. Your problems with a back order, mail delivery problem, or product problem are not the customer's concern. It is up to you to figure out a way to keep the customer happy and want to continue to do business with you.

Then prepare your solution:
>   o   Do you understand the problem?
>   o   Decide what you can do to stand behind your product
>   o   How can you rectify the problem and/or make concessions?
>   o   Establish how far you can and should go to solve the issue

If your customer is telling you about a problem, it is a VERY big deal to them. Most people do not actually tell a salesperson how unhappy they are with a product. They are actually giving you a chance to keep them as a customer. Something about you or the product has made them give you a chance to make it right. They obviously want to continue a business relationship with you. So do not fight with them; make it right.

When a customer needs to vent, tell you the story behind a problem, or an objection to the opportunity you presented, listen courteously and with active interest. This makes her feel understood and give you insight into the problem. Sometimes it is not at the surface. You need to do some digging. When you ask questions, you let the customer know you listened and are clarifying what you heard. Sometimes this is the key to solving the problem or overcoming the objection to hosting a party or even joining your company.

A complaining customer can be your worst enemy but if you handle the situation correctly, she is a potential walking advertisement for you and your company. Take advantage of the opportunity. Remember your best advertisement is word of mouth. You want that word to be good. A satisfied customer who had a complaint or problem that you fixed is your best fan.

Years ago, I was working on the phone prospecting for new parties. A lady I contacted began a tirade about how terrible the company was. Being new, I had never experienced anything but positive feedback about my company. I listened and finally realized the root of her tirade. She had received a defective piece and the consultant never replaced it.

The piece cost $1.50. I knew the company honored defectives and even if they had not, the cost certainly was not the problem. The consultant had not taken the time to tend to the little things associated with her business. The consultant should have taken the 10 or 15 minutes it takes to report a defective or missing piece to the company. Instead, she probably procrastinated and consequently, forgot about it. But the customer did not forget about it and the longer it went unresolved the bigger the problem seemed.

I had the woman tell me exactly what she needed and I purchased the piece. I brought it to her. When she realized why I was at her home, she asked, "Why did you do that? There is nothing in it for you!" She did not realize how much I gained that day.

I now had a very loyal customer who sung my praises anytime she had a chance. Although, she did not feel she wanted to host a party at that time, she gave me some names of friends. These hostesses started chains of parties in groups I never would have had otherwise. I held many parties, earned lots of money and even found one consultant to join our company. Most importantly, I felt good about making someone happy and she no longer told everyone that my company was horrible.

We all know that the customer is not always right but the point is not to place blame but to retain your customer. Do not argue with him/her. Unbelievably a third of all problems with merchandise are caused by the customer themselves.

At one of my parties in the first 6 months of my sales career, I had a customer who brought me a defective bowl. She had quite obviously used the product incorrectly. Our warranty did not cover use in the microwave in 1986) and I informed her of this. She loudly proclaimed she had NOT put it in the microwave-- even though I could see burnt pits in the bottom of the bowl from hot corn kernels.

I did not know how to handle her. I brought the bowl to my distributor so she could enlighten me how to tell the lady we could not replace it. I thought she would have some sage words for me to tell the woman. She simply said, "Give her a new one."

I almost fell over. I said, "But you can tell by looking at the bowl that she popped popcorn in the microwave and the kernels burnt the bottom!" My distributor agreed. "So why give her a new one?" I asked. That is when I received some wise advice.

She said, "Although we both know she misused the product, we need to solve the problem. If we do not replace this bowl, this lady continues to rant and rave about our terrible warranty. No one realizes she caused the problem; they only hear her side of the story and sympathize with her. The amount the bowl costs is a small price to pay for customer satisfaction. One unhappy customer spreads more bad press than 10 happy customers.
Order the bowl."

******The goal is to solve the problem******

Always thank them for giving you the opportunity to help them. You want them to feel as if this was part of your job and you are not being put out by tending to the problem. You want them to leave the experience thinking, "Wow that was the best customer service I ever experienced. I will definitely do business with her again."

With all the retailers, wholesalers, and internet sites a customer has to do business with, growth of your business can begin to slow or even stagnate. Your secret weapon is customer service. Follow up to make sure the customer is satisfied. Nothing is worse than a problem that continues to be unresolved. If you think you had an irate customer before, it is nothing compared to a customer who continues to have the same unresolved problem.

The reason you want to retain customers and hostesses is not only that it is the right thing to do, it is also profitable. Time is money and losing customers is wasteful. When you retain your customer base, you are saving precious time and money. You will not have to replace this income. You can spend your time adding income by increasing not replacing your customer base. The amount of money to acquire a customer is your customer acquisition cost and you want this to be as minimal as possible.

Satisfied Customers:
> Create repeat business
> Lower the time and money costs for replacement
> Usually have higher sales than new customers do
> Refer friends and family

Bottom line: Satisfied Customers = Higher Profits!!!!!

Now you have found customers, given them great customer service, continued to solve their problems and improved your business. Now you have to make sure that you are foremost in their minds. The only way to assure your hostesses think of you first, is to have a consistent, positive rapport with her. There are numerous products in the market place from which she can choose. You are not just competing with other party plans, you are in direct competition with stores, mail order, and internet sites. You need to make sure she thinks of your product first. Retail stores and internet businesses do not give her free product for purchasing and having her friends purchase as well.

Do not lose your hostesses and customers due to inattention. Call them periodically when new merchandise or catalogs are introduced. If you do not see or talk to them for a few months, do a courtesy call to find out how they are doing or would like to host a party to see the new products. Maintain contact and encourage relationships. Protect your investment in your customers by letting them know that they are a very vital part of your business.

Ways to Maintain Contact:

Send out emails, texts and post on social media: When your company introduces new products or has specials, get the information to your customers.

Mail Thank you notes: Always send your hostess a thank you for hosting a party with you. Handwrite your correspondence. Never underestimate the power of a thank you. It is one of the easiest ways to keep you unforgettable and respected. How many people do you know that write a thank you ? What do you feel like when you do receive one?

Remember Preferences: Keeping a notebook of hostess and guest preferences can give you the perfect opportunity to contact them. When a new item that you think would interest them is introduced, you have the perfect opportunity to make a call to them. It is a compliment to them that you are interested in them. Most people do not know any more about their customer than what they purchased.

Host Special Recognition Parties: I hold these at least twice a year. I take pictures of them and email one to them. They are very proud of their accomplishments and usually show off the photo to all their friends----Free advertising!

Technology has made customer service an even bigger challenge. Customers are very informed. They can research products and prices on the Internet for their needs. They comparison shop. Today's customers are not intimidated by salespeople and often know as much about the product as they do.

So what can you do? The competition can copy product, pricing and warranty but they cannot duplicate you. You are the best defense against the competition. Make sure your customers know how much you value their business and appreciate them as a person. Happy customers do not go searching for other places to do business. It is not all about the money. Technology can never replace the human contact. It really is about human relationships.

Chapter 9
Attitude is Everything

A positive mental attitude is the difference between success and failure. Your attitudes toward the product, the work required and how successful you wish to be are all directly affected by your attitude. Decide that you have the power to control most situations. Sometimes controlling it may mean realizing you should change direction. Take responsibility for where you are now and where you are headed. You alone are responsible for how you handle any obstacle in your path to success.

A top notch salesperson starts each day with renewed optimism. No matter how bad the prior day, an upbeat, confident attitude wipes the slate clean. All salespeople experience their share of ups and downs. It is how you handle the challenging situations that determine your level of success.

7 Steps to a New Attitude:
    1.) Develop a Positive Attitude
    2.) Eliminate Blame—Accept Responsibility
    3.) Find your Burning Desire
    4.) Do what you do Better
    5.) Keep the Momentum Going
    6.) Think outside the Box
    7.) Don't QUIT!!!!

Develop a Positive Outlook

Positive salespeople expect a positive outcome. They do not hope. They KNOW! They project a confident attitude-- "I know what I am doing. I am successful." Customers and other salespeople are drawn to them. Salespeople want to learn everything possible from them. Increased sales are a result of a positive mentality.

Make a conscious effort to associate with the most positive people in your organization. They are currently or are likely to become, the most successful salespeople in the company. You learn from them and naturally start to look at the positive side of the business. Positive people project confidence and others are naturally drawn to them. They listen attentively, work on relationships, and understand how to function in almost any conditions. They know when to step back and when to change directions. A positive person garners respect and admiration from those around him/her.

BAD ATTITUDE = NEGATIVE RESULTS
GOOD ATTITUDE = POSITIVE RESULTS
GREAT ATTITUDE = EXCEPTIONAL RESULTS

There are times when your attitude turns negative and pessimistic. This usually accompanies a drop in business or a bad experience. When you face a difficult situation, your first instinct is to run away from it or blame someone. Those who do not give in to this instinct are the people who look for possibilities in even the most adverse situations. There are many who do not finish. Some quit in the very beginning; others quit as the road becomes steeper and more difficult to climb. The most successful sales people are the ones who have hit numerous obstacles and have learned how to maneuver around or through them.

A continued negative attitude eventually destroys your business. Negativity is contagious. If you surround yourself with defeatist people who constantly complain, soon, you adopt the same mindset. Do not associate with negativity or project it yourself. Evaluate the people you associate with. Does this person pull me up or push me down? Make a decision to improve your attitude.

When I was promoted to sales manager another girl, Sally, promoted at about the same time. No matter what I did, I never seemed to be able to come close to what she was achieving. Almost effortlessly, her group sold enough for her to be in the top five sales positions in the distributorship and she always received

*the top new manager award each week. Her group sold amazing
amounts of product. Any goal the distributor challenged us to do,
she met and usually exceeded.*

*Sally was a shooting star. Unfortunately, a shooting star
shines for a while and then falls, which is exactly what happened
to her.*

*As her sales dropped, so did her attitude. What once was a
great company now had an endless list of faults. She made excuses
and blamed anything and anyone except herself. At first, I listened
and sympathized. Then one day I realized I was becoming one of
her negative followers. I made a choice to go look for the positive
sales people.*

*Eventually, Sally faded into the sunset. Inevitably, in sales,
peaks turn into valleys. If you learn how to handle these obstacles,
you are better equipped to ride out the valleys and start up the
path to the peak again. Sally rose too quickly and easily. She hit
the bottom hard and could not get up.*

*I continued to learn, and keep a positive attitude. My group
began to grow and sales improved as well. I found I had built a
solid foundation and knew how to ride the waves of up and down
sales. When my personal or group performance fell, I talked to
other managers for inspiration and experience. I used the
knowledge I acquired from the school of hard knocks. Most
importantly, I kept going! My attitude occasionally faltered but I
always found my way back.*

Negative people project distrust and blame. The biggest
difference between a negative person and a positive one is that a
negative person thinks of only one person---themselves. They talk
about others and use them to their advantage.

Once you move from a negative to a positive outlook, you
feel lucky. Positive people are not lucky. They have the same
obstacles, low points, and problems as anyone else in the
organization. Positive people just choose to rise above the
obstacles and find a solution. Luck is a four-letter word spelled
W-O-R-K.

Developing a positive habit is not easy. It easy to suggest you have a positive outlook on everything, but it is harder to implement, especially if you are not naturally easy going. If you know where your weaknesses lie, you can overcome them. and move on, you direct your energy in a positive direction.

A valuable positive habit to develop is the practice of acting instead of reacting. Reacting is matching your attitude to an aggressor's. Acting is deciding how you wish the conversation to go.

A disgruntled customer calls and starts to rant and rave about a problem with you or your company. She attacks you with insults and accusations. Most of them are not true and you find yourself becoming increasing irritated as she continues her rampage. Probably she has gotten to this level of agitation because no one has listened to her or solved the problem.

If you react, you snap back at the person, matching her anger and escalating the problem. Usually It ends with nothing resolved and a very angry customer. In addition, the customer is armed with another episode to add to the story and no resolution in sight.

If you act, you try to diffuse the situation by remaining even-tempered. You listen to the problem in its entirety and ask questions to try and discover the root of the anger and frustration. Most people respond to a calm voice by bringing down their voice level at least a few notches. The longer you remain calm, the better chance there is for a conversation, not a shouting match. Your goal is to decompress the situation.

If you can empathize with the problem, most times a mutual solution is found. When you remain composed, both of you win. Keep this in mind every time you are faced with an adverse situation either with a customer or another sales person: Am I reacting or acting? If you keep reminding yourself to act, it becomes as natural as conversation. With your new habit you now keep a positive outlook and learn from your mistakes.

Eliminate Blame from your World

A great salesperson takes personal responsibility for not only the success they have but the failures as well. They use them as learning experiences and understand the value of obstacles. Even when the blame rests on the company or another person, a great salesperson does not worry about why it happened or who did it, she directs their energy toward a solution. Blaming wastes precious time and energy. Blaming is a negative emotion and is not conducive to a growing, thriving business.

You are not going to change what already transpired. People who disengage from adverse situations avoid further discouragement, but they also miss out on all the joy that can and does follow a triumph. The key is not to give up. When we review our life, we realize it is the hurdles we overcome that make us stronger.

For almost my entire sales career, I have lived and worked in rural areas. I learned there are some definite advantages as well as disadvantages to selling in either rural or city settings. You cannot blame lack of sales on living in a particular area.

My first six weeks in sales were spent in a small, rural distributorship. At one of our weekly meetings, we discovered our distributorship must merge with the city distributorship two hours away. Many, including myself, believed we could never compete with the city sales. I had been the top new consultant for all of those six weeks. With the increased amount of consultants, I felt defeated before I had hardly started my new career.

Our top manager announced she was finished and would certainly NOT drive that distance for a meeting. Most of the managers agreed with her. They felt their sales would plummet and that the city managers had a distinct advantage over our small sales force. If all the established managers thought this merger a disaster, how would I survive?

One salesperson, Dick, had experience selling products in numerous sales organizations. He listened quietly to our concerns. His career spanned over twenty years. He survived leadership changes, restructuring, economy shifts and company dissolutions. This challenge paled in comparison to some of his experiences. He knew about the peaks, valleys and struggles associated with a party plan career.

After the discussion, he took me aside and said this to me, "They are people just like you. They are no better or worse. Sales can be found anywhere if you look. Just keep doing what you have been doing and you will be on stage with them." I secretly doubted his advice but decided to give it a few weeks before I made a decision.

The merger went on as planned. The first few meetings were rough. We drove the two hours to the new distributorship every Monday. We knew very few people and chose to stick close to our little group. Almost a third of our former small group slowly disappeared. Our attitudes were less than desirable and we felt like the small fish in a big pond.

Slowly we found our footing, made new contacts and started to shine. We found new friends and learned new techniques. With the larger sales force, came more managers from which to learn ideas. Suddenly, I was on stage for top sales for the week! I found out that I could compete with the city sales force. It does not matter where you live, people buy product. You may have to travel greater distances or develop different sales techniques but persistence pays off in rural as well as city atmospheres.

Some of those sales people from our small distributorship left the company, blaming the merger for their failure. Those who did not blame the company eventually succeeded; sometimes even surpassed previous sales levels. Competition was stiffer but the reward of being top sales person in that environment was equally more rewarding.

Dick was right. You can justify any reason for your failure. Success is when you overcome the obstacles and persevere. He had worked in rural and city areas. He supported 6 children on a career in sales and he was a man in a dominantly female organization. Not once did I ever hear him blame lack of sales on his circumstances. He always said,

"The only person you can blame for your success or your failure is YOU!"

Eventually salespeople who blame everyone and anything for their failures are not part of the group. No one wants to associate with a person who may foist blame on them. They do not cultivate relationships and are indifferent to others. They do not bond or create friendly competitions. Usually, there is no plan and no goal. They establish the attitude of isolation and self-pity. They wallow in it.

Eliminate blame, take responsibility and then:

Find your Burning Desire

To become an extraordinary salesperson, you need to find your burning desire. Burning desire is the unquenchable urge to succeed regardless of the obstacles. It is what separates the good from the great. In order to find your burning desire, you need to spend time improving all areas of your business. One skill usually dominates the rest. It may be to be top in sales, leadership, or recruiting. Your job is to find out what lights your inner fire.

In sales, there are always reward levels to strive for. It can be travel, a car, gifts or cash. Most organizations have personal and group levels that are rewarded in some way as well as recruiting and development. When you find something you love, make it your passion. Do not let any obstacle stop you. Burning desire should be like a wildfire out of control. Anything in your path should be overcome.

One company I worked for offered travel as an incentive for higher sales levels. As a new consultant, you had a three-year sales goal instead of the normal one-year to earn a trip to Hawaii. It was a very reachable goal for anyone who wished to go. I went to Hawaii but the sales required to earn a yearly trip seemed insurmountable. How could I ever do the same amount needed to go on a trip in one year? I had kids, a job and lots of excuses!

My consultant friend insisted we go for it. She gave me all the reasons why we should try to go to Bangkok and the excitement of being in Hawaii made it desirable. Suddenly, I wanted to go on that trip the following year. I had the burning desire to go to Bangkok with everyone else.I came home and started to date parties like a crazy woman. I would do two on a Saturday and date two on weeknights---one to do and one to sell. If one cancelled I always had one left. I was rarely without a party. When some cancelled, I booked more. My consultants loved my overbooking strategy. The times I had both hold on a night, one of my consultants did it for me and earned extra money.

I found creative ways to sell more in one party. I offered the double hostess option. I promoted fundraisers by going schools and clubs. I held multiple hostess bingos.

I earned the trip to Bangkok and every trip offered after that. I realized that it is possible when you have a burning desire to make it happen. All these party options were always available; I just did not have the desire to utilize them.

Your burning desire may change. It does not have to remain the same each month or each year. Sometimes once you accomplish a goal, you need to find a new one. You need to keep the spark. If the spark is gone so is the burning desire. When the burning desire dies, success starts to slip. If you do not rekindle the flame, your success eventually dies with it.

Do what you do better

Once you have worked to achieve success, you cannot rest on your laurels Successful salespeople continue to do what they are already doing. They just do it better. Competition forces you to be the best you can be. You must do what you do even better than you did before. You develop better sales techniques and unequalled customer service. Friendly competition is very healthy. Everyone involved reaches heights they would not normally attain. Competition is how consultants, managers, and the company grow.

So how do you continue to expand and grow? Goals. Goals keep you focused. They are also a way to measure your success. As you reach a goal and set a new one, you know exactly where you are and where you are headed. To make something happen, you have to plan it. Think about this: A mind is like a sweater; once it's stretched, it can never go back.

Keep the Momentum Going—Get Motivated!

Sales without motivation has no momentum. Superior sales require superior motivation. Motivation requires knowledge of the business, a reward system, and a support person/group. Even with all of these elements, the commitment to success and the business is essential. Staying motivated is a conscious decision and it is definitely not easy.

Motivation requires a reward of some kind. Rewards are either tangible or intangible. Many companies not only present gifts and rewards for the top salespeople, they have a multitude of levels for everyone to strive for. Companies realize they need to inspire the newest members as well as the top salespeople. Gifts can range from small items to cars and trips. Once a person achieves a small goal, it is only natural to strive for the next level and the next. Slowly, and sometimes without the person realizing it, the company pulls them up to higher levels of sales and recruiting.

In addition to the tangible rewards, there is another, sometimes, more inspirational kind of reward. It is the intangible reward or the glory reward. It satisfies one of humans' more basic needs---Acceptance and Respect. There is no measure for this reward. Most sales companies know this is far more important to most people than the money or gifts they offer. Some gifts received for goals achieved sometimes seem almost small in relation to the amount of effort required to achieve it. To the inexperienced person, it is hard to understand what motivates a salesperson to strive to be #1 for these seemingly insignificant items. These rewards are the tangible reminder of the goal achieved.

The biggest reward is the pride in achieving a top status in the company is standing before your peers. No matter whether it is a school child going on stage to receive a piece of paper stating his/her superior grade point average, or a salesperson accepting a top category award, the satisfaction is in the accomplishment. There is no price tag big enough for this kind of achievement.

Maintaining motivation is the hardest part of the equation. When you are at a sales meeting or any other motivational class, it is easy to get excited and want to go out and conquer the world. However, the world also wants to conquer you and maintaining a positive attitude is not always easy. Only a small percentage of people can maintain motivational excitement on their own. Even then, it takes a lot of work and persistence. Repeated exposure to any motivational event, meeting, or group get together is crucial to your continued success.

One year four of us chose to drive the 25 hours to get to the national sales meeting. Flights were expensive and our sales had not been enough to justify the cost of an airline ticket to Florida. We knew we needed to go so we chose the least expensive option which was to drive, split the gas costs and bring a cooler full of food.

When we made the decision to drive instead of fly, we never realized what a business changing decision it would turn out to be. On the way down all we could talk about was how badly our sales and groups were doing. All we could see was the negative side of the business.

But something happened at the sales meeting. We attended training that focused on building group and individual sales. We talked to many successful managers and listened to their sage advice. As the excitement grew and the stories began to unfold of personal perseverance and amazing results, something changed in our attitudes. Instead of "I'll never be able to do that", it was "I can do that!!"

All the way home, we discussed our plans to keep our motivation going. How we could keep each other and our teams going. We both were in danger of losing our cars if our group sales did not improve, but were motivated to keep them. We had just witnessed what was possible and intended to make it happen for ourselves.

The first thing we knew we needed to do was motivate each other so we devised a plan of friendly weekly competition. Each week at our morning meeting, we created a different goal. Some weeks it was sales and others it was recruiting. The loser treated the winner to lunch. Neither of us wanted to be the loser, so we worked very hard each week. It was a great motivator. We were helping each other as well as building our groups. Our sales began to climb.

Recruiting became my focus. Soon I was recruiting and training constantly. Where had all these people been before? I had not been focused or motivated enough to recruit them. As an individual, I could only sell a certain amount but with a group of salespeople, the sky was the limit. Initially, my personal sales plummeted, but the time I took to recruit and train new people was time well spent. Eventually, my group sales increased and my efforts rewarded.

Here is where a strange phenomenon happened. Where I had been focused on my sales and group performance for me, I found myself concerned with their individual success. My success became a by-product of that. The group realized I really cared about them and their success. Everyone worked together and usually surpassed our weekly and monthly goals.

People must be motivated to excel and, in turn, motivate the people working for them or around them. Motivation works the best when the people involved want to help you attain greatness. Genuine caring and respect of both parties involved is a vital part of motivation. If a person does not feel valued, nothing motivates them. Harry Truman said it best, "It is amazing what you can accomplish if you don't care who gets the credit." When you stop focusing on me and start thinking us, success follows.

Individual assessment uncovers each person's hot button. For some, it is rewards such as gifts or money; others react better to recognition and praise; while still others need the respect of their peers. Ultimately, you cannot understand the impact of your motivation/reward system until you understand the individual members of your team.

Many people do not give motivation the importance that they do other qualities in management. When highly successful companies are researched, most of them have highly motivated workers and an above average reward system. From my experience, I believe that motivation should be at the top of the list of management qualities. Motivated people can achieve levels that seem unattainable. Reaching a goal is 10% knowledge and 90% attitude. A motivated attitude can shatter records.

Think Outside the Box

In order to learn something new, you need to step outside of your comfort zone, think outside the box, and try new ideas. Be receptive to a new way of thinking and a new way of doing something. Evaluate its merits and drawbacks. You may decide not to continue or you may find a great new adventure. The key is to be open to change. Sometimes very drastic change. The daring people who step outside of their comfort zones, usually grow and succeed. Mistakes are all right. Not taking a chance is worse than making the wrong choice. It is not how many times you fall, but how many times you get back up that makes the difference.

No matter what you do personally or in business, you cannot grow until you stretch yourself to do something you have not done before. It needs to scare you a little. Initially, you may need to start with small changes. Over time, you will naturally progress to bigger, more challenging things. Without realizing it, you grow a little with each task you undertake no matter what the outcome.

Here are some Outside the Box exercises you can try:

- o Make one call to a stranger or distant acquaintance to book a party
- o Work a craft fair and talk to as many people as possible
- o Shadow another consultant or manager
- o Attend a workshop about something you know very little about
- o Role play with another dating parties or recruiting
- o Give a training talk on a subject you are passionate about

When I promoted to manager, part of the job required managers to prepare a teaching seminar every 6-8 weeks. I could not understand how I would have anything to offer all those managers who had been in sales for twenty years or more. New managers, maybe, but definitely not the experienced ones!

Even if I possessed infinite wisdom which these managers could use, I would have to speak in front of my peers which still scared me. I only recently adjusted to the demonstrations I gave at parties. Now, as a manager, I would be required to speak in front of my sales associates.

I talked with the distributor to challenge this rule. I informed her that if I had realized that talking in front of the entire sales force was part of a manager's job, I would have declined the offer. She responded, "Good thing we didn't tell you about the fine print." I further argued that even if I felt comfortable doing it, I would have nothing to offer the managers and seasoned consultants. The distributor told me that everyone had a different style of selling, recruiting and training. I would be surprised.

With a shaky voice, and even shakier knees I walked to the podium to give my talk. Afterward, two managers approached me and expressed interest in a couple of my ideas. I do not know if they were being kind, but in any case, it raised my confidence tremendously.

Years passed and I became one of those seasoned managers. At one of our weekly meetings I realized I was listening to a new manager's talk and taking notes. Sometimes it takes a while to understand that you are learning. I, now, truly believed that everyone has something to convey.

Do Not Quit

The most important attitude to adopt is **DO NOT QUIT!** After all the time and effort you have expended to make your business a success, if you quit, it all becomes wasted time. A sales career is like a roller coaster ride, a series of intense highs with periodic drops. Just like a roller coaster, you do not stay at the top or the bottom forever. If you realize the lows are part of the business, you start to accept them as a challenge rather than a defeat.

Understanding the logistics of the sales business does not make the setbacks any easier. When you are in the doldrums, your problems seem insurmountable. Depression and negativity try to

take over your business life. It can seem easier to quit than go on.
And it is easier to quit. A victor is not looking for the easier road.
She is looking for the successful one.

Sales inevitably falter or drop. Sometimes it is an
unavoidable event in your life, an economy shift, a temporary loss
of interest in your product, or just a cyclical slump. Whatever the
reason, a top salesperson finds a solution. Anyone selling for an
extended period of time knows there are always peaks and valleys
and the valleys can often be VERY deep.

The old adage says, "When the going gets tough, the tough
get going." Tough times and tough markets show the true colors
of a salesperson. It is easy to be a top seller in a prime market but
true champions weather the rocky road and do not quit. It calls for
creativity and a positive attitude. Leaders expect to make it
through the hard times and look for solutions and alternative
methods. They launch a new game plan and experiment with new
ideas.

It may be necessary to double or even triple your
networking by working craft fairs or events to gather leads or even
trying a new avenue such as friend finding. Increase the
frequency that you contact hostesses and ask for referrals. Try new
party alternatives. At this point, something needs to change. If
you continue on the same path, eventually it becomes a dead end.
Reinvent yourself, revitalize your business, and accept change.
Salespeople who resist change, fail to see the chance to grow from
the experience and miss the opportunity to rise above failure and
truly succeed!

DON'T QUIT

When things go wrong, as they sometimes will,
When the road you're trudging is all uphill,
When the funds are low, and the debts are high,
And you want to smile, but you have to sigh,
When care is pressing you down a bit,
Rest if you must, but don't you quit.

Life is strange with its twists & turns,
As everyone of us sometimes learns,
And many a failure turns about when he might have won
Had he stuck it out:
Don't Give up tho the pace seems slow,
You may succeed with another blow.

Often the goal is nearer than it seems to a faint and faltering man
Often the struggler had given up,
When he might have captured the victor's cup.
And he learned too late, when the night slipped down,
How close he was to the golden crown.

Success is failure turned inside out,
The silver tint of clouds of doubt,
And you never know how close you are,
It may be near when it seems so far
So stick to the fight when you're hardest hit,
It's when things seem worse,
That you must not **QUIT**............
Author Unknown

Chapter 10
Grow & Expand

Every company must grow and expand. Generally, this means hiring new people. There are many different names used for it: Sharing the opportunity, Recruiting, Sponsoring... Quite simply it is offering another person the chance to do what you do. For our purposes, let's call it recruiting. Recruiting is a skill you develop. But top recruiting is a feeling that comes from the heart. Once you really believe in the business you have chosen, you want to tell everyone you meet about it. When you truly love what you do, it is not convincing someone to try it, it is offering them a wonderful opportunity for a fun and rewarding career.

Although recruiting skills develop with time and practice, it is your attitude that draws people to you more than the words you choose. It is probably the hardest habit to establish for beginning and even veteran sales people. As with most things, it is all about your mindset. When you recruit someone within the first thirty days of your career you are more likely to make it a habit. Usually, you are so excited about your new career that you talk, talk, and talk about your new endeavor to everyone. You do not have to know all the logistics of your new career, just be enthusiastic about it. People are drawn to your positive energy and start asking questions. As time goes by, you learn more and more about the company and how to answer many of their questions but, remember, enthusiasm recruits more people than facts.

When I am talking to a hostess to close her party I say "Have you ever considered doing what I do?" Then I listen!! If you are a consultant, you have several options; ask permission for your manager to contact her, call your manager right then and have her talk to your potential recruit, or simply invite her to the next event to check it out.

As a consultant, your job is to recommend people you believe would benefit from joining the company to your manager or supervisor. The amount you talk to that person prior to giving her name to your manager is up to the individual consultant and/or the situation. Your manager or supervisor's job is to explain the wonderful opportunities and benefits that are unique and appealing with your company.

Think about why you joined the company and why you love your job. It is no different than finding a real job and telling everyone about it. But in party plan you have a unique situation. You can offer the chance for a job like yours to anyone.

Why should you offer the opportunity?
1.) Most companies offer monetary or gift rewards for recruiting
2.) When you sponsor someone you have a "buddy" in the business with whom you can share experiences and have a friendly competitions
3.) New people always inspire the rest of the group to do better
4.) New people bring new and different ideas to the group
5.) Elevated respect in your group
6.) If you decide to become a manager, your people go with you
7.) Recruiting builds your confidence which in turns makes you a better salesperson.

How to offer the opportunity:
1.) Use drawing slips at your parties and submit all of them to your manager and   let her decide on the potential prospects.
2.) Give the name of someone at the party who asked lots of questions about your job and how you like it.
3.) You can initiate a conversation with someone you feel would be a great consultant and ask if your manager could contact her
4.) Tell a story at the party about how you started and why you love it
5.) Love what you do—it will show what a great job you have

Even if you don't think you want to advance, recruiting is a great way to add more people, knowledge, and fun to your group. It creates camaraderie and friendly competition. If you ever do decide to advance to management, your people follow you to your own group.

You should explore the possibilities of advancement by attending an informational meeting. It does not cost you anything except some time to explore options. If you decide advancement is not for you, you still acquired more valuable knowledge to help you in your business.

The best part about recruiting is that all you have to do is give your manager names of people who would be great consultants. She does the work for you. She contacts these potential recruits, sets up an appointment for an interview, and ensures the new consultants are properly trained. If you desire, you can accompany her on the interview to watch the procedure and learn how to do a recruit interview yourself.

Sometimes you cannot seem to pick out someone at the party. Many times this skill comes with practice so you need a few tricks until you become more confident offering the opportunity. Many of these ideas you continue to use even after you become proficient at recruiting.

One of these methods is the drawing form. I have drawing forms that I use at parties to help me target people to interview. I use these to set up interviews. As a consultant, it is an easy way to find potential new people. All you have to do is pass them out with the catalogs and do a drawing with them at the end of the demonstration. Then you hand the ones you think are good leads to your manager.

Another way to find leads is to play games that specifically target hiring new people. If you are doing the auction party, near the end of the demonstration, ask for 5 people to ask anything about your job and they will receive an extra $100. This is an excellent window into people's thinking and you can listen for questions like "How much is your kit?' "How many nights do you work a week?"

A game called the Kiss Game also works on the same premise. Most people love chocolate and are enticed to ask questions to get a Hershey's Kiss. Every person who asks a question directly related to your job gets one. After she asks the question and you answer, throw her a kiss. Guests start to ask all kinds of questions just to get a chocolate.

Pay attention to the questions asked and who asks them. Some great questions may lead to a new consultant for you.

If you become a manager, you set up the interviews for your consultants and yourself. When calling to set up an interview say, "I really enjoyed meeting you last night or (Kathy highly recommended you) and I'd love to show you the wonderful opportunities in _____. You may not be interested now but I need to see 5 people a week. There's no obligation. It only takes about 15-20 min. and I'm in your neighborhood anyway tomorrow about 10:00. You're at 22 Knox Street? Could I stop by around 10 and do a quick interview with you?" If they say yes, stop selling the opportunity and say "Great! I'll see you at 10!"

At the Interview:
✓ Sell enough benefits for her
✓ Justify why it would be good for her and her family
✓ Find 2 reasons why you think it would be good for her
✓ Make sure you have a step by step plan
✓ Keep a positive attitude
✓ Show confidence in her and her ability to do it
✓ Listen to objections and discuss solutions

Closure is very important. Normally, if they say they'll think about it, you've lost them. Even if the person is still considering the opportunity, date a party with her. Your goal from every recruit interview is to at least to come away with a party. What you can say to her if she is wavering is this, "How about we just get started with a little get-together of your friends? They can see the product and decide if they would like to help you get started in your new business. If you decide not to do this, the worst thing to happen would be we have a regular party and you get some free merchandise. That would be all right wouldn't it?" Very few people turn that down.

Parties are the best place for recruit leads but I also get them everywhere I go. I listen for the same things I do at a party. I have recruited consultants from other states, drawing slips, phone calls, leads, and update calling. I have found consultants in stores, at kids' functions and school PTA. I have even recruited people from other party plans when what I have to offer is better than their current party plan.

The most important thing I learned when targeting people is never discount anyone. One of the hardest obstacles to overcome in recruiting is prejudging people's situation or ability to do the job. You eventually learn to target certain people but you must try never to mentally dismiss someone. You do not know what a person's true feelings or situation are. If you think they lack a quality, they may very well have enough other great attributes to make a great consultant.

Sharon was a hostess for me. She had an average party with one party dated from her party. She had 7 children ranging from Kindergarten to 12th grade. She held down a full time job, and through her own admission, had a less than helpful husband. In my mind, she was not a great prospect for a new consultant in my group.

The new party she had from her party was a young girl that was friends with her oldest daughter. She was in college and needed money. The party was pretty small. In fact, the only people in attendance were the hostess, Alexis, one of her friends, Sharon and me. Alexis was full of enthusiasm. I thought she was perfect fit — young, excited, and needed money.

I began to tell Alexis the benefits of my great job. I told her about the flexible hours and the good hourly wage. I showed her pictures of the gifts I had earned and how I drove a company car. Sharon sat and listened. Alexis was ready to sign the papers when Sharon spoke up and said, "Could I try this too?"

I was shocked and embarrassed. I also realized how judgmental I had been. In my mind, I thought it would be a

complete waste of time and energy for both of us. I was about to
learn a valuable lesson!

Sharon talked to 6 of her friends and they held her initial
parties in record time. She was my top consultant within a couple
of months and stayed top consultant for months. She became my
first consultant who promoted to manager.

Alexis? She never finished dating her initial parties. She
held 2 parties and turned her kit back in.

I had another learning experience a few years later. It was
a totally different scenario but it was equally as judgmental.

I had just moved to a new area 3 hours from where I used
to live and do business. I would have to build a whole new group.
As I was in the middle of relocating, a recruit lead was given to me
by the office. I later learned two other managers had turned down
the lead.

The office told me she was very excited and lived ten
minutes from me. So far so good. Then the bomb. Lydia had no
phone and no car. The office encouraged me to just go talk with
her.

I called her and scheduled an interview. Lydia was a really
nice person and insisted she could make it work. She had enough
enthusiasm! I decided I did not have much to lose except some
time and the lead had materialized through the main office so... I
signed her up. Against, my better judgment—I thought.

Her introductory party was almost a complete failure.
Only one person showed up and the sales were not even at the
entry level to consider it a party. I figured that was the end of that
fiasco. Lydia would not give up even when her efforts to date her
first 5 parties took weeks. Finally, she had her party line-up and
she was ready to go.

She had a message phone for people to call and several
friends who brought her to her parties with their cars. A couple of
her parties were with people in the neighborhood. She walked,
carrying her kit, to these. I had never seen such perseverance in

my life. No matter what obstacles were placed in front of Lydia, she found a way through, over, or around them!

Slowly, she emerged as a consistent salesperson. Money came in and she installed a phone and then bought an old car. Soon she was doing tremendous selling. She was the top performer in my group. At our regional sales meeting, she was honored as a top consultant.

In both of these cases, the odds were against them succeeding or even finishing the requirement of 5 parties to earn the kit. They had enough drive and enthusiasm to overcome their obstacles. Attitude is everything! I learned valuable lessons that I have never forgotten. I do not judge when recruiting and try my best to look past the outside into the attitude and enthusiasm bubbling below the surface.

Once you have a recruiting attitude you find it easier and easier to spot people to offer the opportunity. Your positive attitude also makes people begin to ask you questions about your job. They see you having a great time and the more successful you seem, the more curious they are about your job.

Your best recruiting tool is YOU.
- Talk about your job and they can tell you love it
- Trips experiences from your company spark interest
- Bring a potential consultant to a rally or meeting
- A filled datebook shows them how successful you are

Eventually I found a button that said it all. I began to wear it everywhere and it truly became my mantra.

I LOVE WHAT I DO---YOU CAN TOO!!!

A WOMAN'S PLACE IS IN SALES!